THIS
IS LEARNING
EXPERIENCE
DESIGN

What it is, **how** it works, and **why** it matters.

Niels Floor

This is Learning Experience Design:
What it is, how it works, and why it matters.
Niels Floor

New Riders
www.peachpit.com
Copyright © 2023 by Pearson Education, Inc. or its affiliates. All Rights Reserved.

New Riders is an imprint of Pearson Education, Inc.
To report errors, please send a note to errata@peachpit.com

Executive Editor: Laura Norman
Development Editor: Margaret S. Anderson
Senior Production Editor: Tracey Croom
Technical Editor: Julie Dirksen
Copy Editor: Kim Wimpsett
Compositor: Kim Scott, Bumpy Design
Proofreader: James M. Fraleigh
Indexer: Valerie Haynes Perry
Cover Design: Chuti Prasertsith
Interior Design: Kim Scott, Bumpy Design
Cover Illustrations: Niels Floor

ISBN-13:   978-0-13-795073-7
ISBN-10:   0-13-795073-X

1 2022

To my love Kim Bergmans
for always being there for me.

To my father Aart Floor
for believing in me and my dreams.

Contents

Acknowledgements

Writing a book may sound like a solitary endeavor. In reality, it takes a whole bunch of people to turn a dream into a reality. I'm deeply grateful to all of you, including those mentioned here.

Pearson/New Riders

As a first-time author I had so much to learn. Laura Norman, you and your colleagues made this book possible. Special thanks to Margaret Anderson for your incredible guidance, Julie Dirksen for your valuable feedback and expertise, and Kim Scott for this beautiful design.

Shapers

We've been through a lot over the years, and I would have never made it this far without you. Your dedication, talent, and friendship mean the world to me. Thank you so much Henna de Koning, Lieke Bremer, Maarten van Broekhoven, Wesselien de Groot, Ron Valstar, Sander Falise, Anne van Egmond, Annemiek Osinga, Katharina Herzog, Fieke Sluijs, and Yuen Yen Tsai.

Learning experience design community

Every day I get to interact with amazing people from around the world who share my passion for learning experience design. I'm grateful for all your support. There are a couple of you I want to thank in particular:

Willem-Jan Renger, you knew pioneering learning experience design was going to be a long and hard road. You stood by me and helped me tremendously along the way. Together with Ina van der Bruq and your colleagues at Utrecht School of the Arts, you have been vital to the development of learning experience design.

Albert Lim at Nanyang Polytechnic in Singapore, thank you for inviting me over and spreading learning experience design in Asia. I truly enjoyed working together with you and your amazing staff including Garry Tan, Shirlyn Goh, Gina Tay, and Annie Ng.

Numerous people have helped with organizing and hosting LXDCON over the years. A big thank-you to Hanneke van den Broek, Rembert Sierksma, Arwen van Putten, Evert Hoogendoorn, Sjoerd Louwaars, Alette Baartmans, Monique Snijder, Leontien van Melle, Daniek Bosch, Frank Léoné, Marco van Hout, Erik Mooij, the incredible volunteers, and all the others who have contributed. Together we spread learning experience design around the globe.

A couple of other wonderful people who have enabled me to do the work I love are Stephanie Kraneveld, Wendy van Eldijk, Tammy Tanumihardja, Katharina Meinert, Adela Georgescu, and Alina Fong.

My family
Kim, Elena, and Annika, I love you more than words can say. Mom, dad, and Sander, I'm blessed to have you in my life.

Preface

The beginning is the most important part of the work.
—PLATO, PHILOSOPHER

Here you are. Reading this book. This could be a pivotal moment in your lifelong learning journey. A journey that started long before you opened this book.

This book is as much about learning experience design (LXD) as it is about you. It is about the next steps that you are going to take in your personal development toward mastering LXD.

Reading this book can help you grasp the fundamentals of LXD. However, reading it is not enough. Once you start to apply, share, and build on what you've learned, the contents of this book will come to life. There is so much to learn from the application of LXD, and the content of this book will put you on the right track.

You may wonder why I chose to write a book on LXD. Isn't LXD all about innovation and using new technologies for state-of-the-art learning experiences? The age of a medium or technology says nothing about its effectiveness. I care about providing a great learning experience using the technology that works best for the goals I want to achieve. Books are tangible, clearly structured, and easily accessible in a way that suits you.

Also, people are different. Some prefer a book where others prefer a video or game. That's why this book is one of several resources that I've created on your path in becoming a learning experience designer.

Another big advantage of writing a book is for the writer. The process of writing this book took many years, and it has helped me immensely to gather and organize my thoughts and to fully understand the concepts of LXD. It forced me to externalize all the ideas and experiences that are floating around in my brain.

Having this book published is more than a personal milestone. It is a marker in the development of LXD as the field of LXD is still relatively unknown and there is a level of confusion on what it is, how it works, and why it matters. I hope this book will provide clarity, meaning, and direction to anyone interested in LXD.

Have a wonderful journey!
Niels Floor

Why read this book?

Enough about me, back to the central figure in this book: you, the reader. Let me ask you a simple question: Why would you read this book?

It may sound redundant to ask you this, but believe me, there are many possible reasons. Maybe you are:

- An instructional designer looking for a new way to find creative solutions for today's educational challenges

- A designer who wants to apply their creative talents and skills to the field of learning

- A teacher looking for ways to increase student engagement and motivation

- A publisher who needs to adapt to a new learning landscape

As you can see, LXD attracts a wide variety of educational and creative professionals. I've learned this from my own experience in applying, teaching, training, and promoting LXD around the globe. I've met, trained, and worked with a colorful bunch of people who have inspired me in writing this book.

Though we may be different, we have at least two things in common: a love for learning and an urge to create better learning experiences. I sincerely believe that this book can help you strengthen your passion for learning and elevate the quality of the experiences you design.

I'm honored to travel with you on your learning journey and to offer you my guidance along the way.

How to read this book

Reading a book is an experience in itself. This book is written and designed with your learning experience in mind.

You might want to prepare for the journey and choose a path that will bring you to the right destination. Here are four options for you to choose from and get you going!

Take a stroll

Casually flip through the pages and stop to look at whatever catches your eye. Don't rush; just see what inspires you and take it from there. Trust your intuition; this can be the start of something unexpected.

This path is ideal if you are new to LXD and you're looking for inspiration.

Where to start:

• Wherever you like, simply start exploring!

Go hiking

Put on a pair of hiking shoes and get off the beaten path. Pick a route and take on the challenges you find along the way. Don't be afraid to take a detour as it might surprise you and lead you to a beautiful viewpoint.

This path is ideal if you are familiar with LXD and you have a general idea of your areas of interest.

Where to start:

- Chapter 2, "Why learning experience design matters"
  A fresh perspective

- Nine rules of learning experience design

- Chapter 3, "What is learning experience design?"
  Defining learning experience design

- Chapter 5, "How to design a learning experience"
  The learning experience design process

- Chapter 6, "The Learning Experience Canvas"
  Introducing the LX Canvas

Take short sprints

You know what you want, and you are ready for action. Select a part that you want to master and go all in for a short period of time.

This path is ideal when you know what you're looking for in LXD and you want to get active straightaway.

Where to start:

- Chapter 6, "The Learning Experience Canvas"

- Chapter 7, "Design tools" (personas, empathy map for learners, experience mapping)

- Chapter 8, "Case studies"

Climb to the top

Take a deep breath and start walking! Simply turn this page, and don't stop until you finish the end of this book. Your perseverance will be rewarded with a beautiful view from the top.

This path is ideal for anyone who wants to build a solid foundation in LXD and is in it for the long run.

Where to start:

- Chapter 1, "The power of experience,"
  The story of the angry boy.

Download LXD resources

Downloadable resources include the Learning Experience Canvas as well as other templates and design tools. To make use of the online content that accompanies this book, just visit your www.peachpit.com account.

You must register your purchase on peachpit.com in order to access the bonus content:

1. Go to **www.peachpit.com/LXDbook** in your web browser.

2. Sign in or create a new account.

3. The ISBN for this book will appear automatically. Click **Submit**.

4. Access the online content from the **Registered Products** tab on your Account page.

If you purchased a digital product directly from peachpit.com, your product will already be registered.

On you go!

The choice is up to you. Whichever path you choose, remember to enjoy the ride!

*No man ever steps in the same
river twice, for it's not the same river
and he's not the same man.*

—HERACLITUS, PHILOSOPHER

The power of experience

IS IN YOUR HANDS

Every single day you have many kinds of experiences. Some are so unnoticeable that you forget them straightaway. Others can instantly turn your world upside down and change your life for good. That's the power of experience, and that power is in your hands.

Experience is highly valued when it comes to our résumés. Any job interview will focus on your prior experience. It's hard to land your dream job without having the right experience. At the same time, education is generally not designed as an experience. It is designed as an educational system. Schools use a systematic approach to facilitate learning in a highly structured, linear manner. This system is based on things such as learning objectives, topics, curricula, rubrics, assessment, quantifiable outcomes, and diplomas. The discrepancy between the complex, unpredictable, and sometimes chaotic reality we live in and the overly organized educational system is striking.

This might explain why the experience of going to school can feel unpersonal, boring, and even frustrating for some students. It is hard to make this systematic approach relatable. The same can apply to professional development. Many of us have clicked through an e-learning course that is predictable and uninspiring, even though, or even because, the content is structured in a logical, orderly, and easily accessible way.

I believe that everybody loves to learn. There is an undeniable intrinsic motivation to learn about things that you care about. People can spend years learning to play an instrument, restoring a classic car, or building a company from the ground up. What would happen when you learn from experiences that excite, engage, and inspire you? That's what this book is about. Let's design some incredible learning experiences!

Designing a learning experience bears responsibility. A responsibility that goes beyond offering instruction or creating content. You are responsible for the complete experience, from beginning to end and beyond. For everything that happens, what the learner does, how it makes them feel, what they learn, and how the outcome affects the learner as a human being.

The choices that you make as a designer and the design you create can have a lasting impact on the learner. Obviously, your goal is to have a positive impact and to provide learners with a memorable experience they appreciate and enjoy. That's easier said than done. I know it can be done, and I've seen great examples of impactful learning experiences. I've created some of those examples. What you need is the perspective, methodology, skills, and tools that enable you to harness the power of experience. Reading this book and applying what you learn will put you on track to do just that.

The story of the angry boy

Once upon a time there was a boy who was very angry. This ill-tempered boy was a menace to his sister and parents. He was always fighting, screaming, and breaking stuff when he got upset.

Unfortunately, the boy got upset easily and often. This is the story of that angry boy.

One day, the father of the angry boy said, "Son, I've got something special for you," and he gave his son a hammer and a box of nails. The boy was confused and asked his father what was special about this hammer. "Well, this hammer is a powerful tool that can really help you," his father responded. "But how?" the boy wondered.

The father asked the boy to come outside into the garden. They were standing in front of their wooden fence when he explained, "The next time you are upset, take this hammer and pound as many nails into this fence as you like."

It didn't take long for the boy to get upset. He grabbed his hammer, ran into the garden, and started pounding nails into the fence. It took a large number of nails before his anger began to dissipate to a point where he was actually calm. He said to himself, "This was OK. I do feel better now."

But not for long. Shortly afterward he became angry once again, so it was off to the garden once more. And many times more in the following days.

As days passed, something struck the boy. Not only was he coming to the fence less often, but he also was using fewer nails than in the beginning. Was he actually becoming less angry?

The boy was proud of his progress, and one day it happened! He called his father into the garden and said, "Dad, yesterday I didn't hit a single nail into the fence!"

His father smiled. "This is cause for a celebration! As a testament to your achievement, each day that you're not angry, you can take one nail out of the fence. And with each nail you take out, remember that I'm truly proud of you and that you should also be proud of yourself."

And so it went. One by one the nails were taken out of the fence. And while it took a long time, that special day arrived when the boy was about to take out the last nail.

"Dad, come here! I've made it!" he yelled. His father watched as his son removed the final nail from the fence.

"I think I've learned my lesson now," the boy said confidently.

"Well, not quite," his father replied. "Take a good look at this fence, and tell me what you see."

The boy looked. "It's full of holes."

"That's right," his father explained. "That's what happens when you hurt someone. It leaves a mark. And you can't just take that away by saying sorry."

His father continued, "Son, please be careful when you feel angry. Just think about this fence before you think about hurting someone."

Lessons learned

The story of the angry boy is a great example of a powerful learning experience. When I first heard this story, I could empathize with the boy and his father. There is a strong connection both on a mental and emotional level.

Analyzing this learning experience will show you some of the core concepts of learning experience design (LXD). So, what makes this such a powerful learning experience for the angry boy?

The father probably wasn't aware of the fact that he applied human-centered design perfectly. He created a learning experience specifically for his son in an empathic and effective way. He knew what his son liked, disliked, and ultimately needed. This knowledge was the foundation for his design.

A good design comes from good ideas. In this case, it was a brilliant and original idea to use the fence as a tool and metaphor that allows the boy to learn insightful lessons. It's an idea that probably works better than any other formal anger management training. It's the quality of his idea and the simplicity of the experience that made it so powerful.

Using a hammer and nails as learning tools is also part of the success. The physical activity of using this age-old technology contributed to relieving anger and crafting a memorable story. Imagine the dad giving the boy a phone with a digital gamified version of hitting nails into a fence. That wouldn't have worked at all. Choosing technology that works is key here.

The learning outcome of this experience goes beyond achieving the objective of managing anger. It is about a profound transformation where the angry boy becomes a happy boy that enjoys life more than ever before. Obviously, the lives of the other family members are improved dramatically. That's a valuable learning outcome for everyone.

There's even more to learn here, but you get the point. A great learning experience works for a specific situation, adds value to people's lives, and lasts a lifetime.

In short, this learning experience:

- Leads to a valuable and meaningful outcome
- Has a lasting positive impact on the learner and his surroundings
- Is human-centered and empathic
- Uses the right technology
- Is a creative, simple, and original solution to a serious problem

These are all core concepts of LXD that will be discussed in more detail throughout this book.

◼ What did you experience?

Let me ask you a personal question. What experience had a profound impact on you? Take a moment to really think about this.

We all have countless experiences, but which one will you remember for the rest of your life? Which experience had a profound and positive impact on you?

Now think about what made this experience so exceptional and memorable. Just like the analysis of the angry boy's story, write down the key qualities of your own experience and what you've learned from it.

As a teacher and trainer, I've asked many people to do this. What's amazing is that each of the answers is a unique story. Some are adventurous like being helped by a kind homeless man in a shady part of a South American city, or going on the road with your favorite band across the United States. Others are about the people you love, like the lack of internet access on a vacation island leading you to strengthen the relationship with your friends through hours of personal conversations.

Sometimes the biggest lessons are learned from sad experiences, like how serious injury can force you to spend your limited energy on the people and things that really matter or how ending up in a foreign hospital allows you to experience a country's beauty and kindness in a non-touristy way. Overcoming obstacles can turn a painful moment into a precious memory.

There are great examples in education as well, like taking a course that kick-starts a new career or having an elementary school teacher who helped you discover your talents and gave you the confidence to develop them. Incredible experiences can happen anywhere and at any time. They can be as simple as enjoying the view at the end of a hike or as complex as completing a four-year master's program.

As diverse as they are, all these experiences have outcomes that matter. You learn something valuable that sticks with you for the rest of your life. These stories are inspirational for the types of experiences we hope to design for others.

Having a good idea of what makes a learning experience great is essential for any (aspiring) learning experience designer. It allows you to set the bar for what you consider to be a well-designed learning experience.

Now that you know the power of experiences, it's time to move forward. Whenever you are in doubt about the quality of your design, just think about your own experience.

If you change the way you look at something, whatever it is you are looking at will change.

— STEVE VAI, MUSICIAN

Chapter 2

Why learning experience design matters

TO YOU AND THE LEARNER

About a decade ago, learning experience design (LXD) was virtually unknown. Recently, that has changed dramatically. Why is that? Let's explore the reasons for this rise in popularity and figure out why LXD matters to you and to the rest of the world.

I've been advocating for LXD since 2007, but it took several years for people to take notice. At first, people simply didn't know or didn't care about it. Basically, when I pitched my ideas for LXD, people were either confused, uninterested, or even agitated. The time simply wasn't right for LXD.

Now, times have changed, and LXD is gaining traction around the world. People are excited about LXD as an alternative way to enable, support, and facilitate learning. LXD has evolved from an idea to an actual design discipline. As LXD evolved, the world changed as well. Today developments inside and outside of LXD are aligning. The world is ready for LXD, and vice versa.

What attracts people to LXD? What made you pick up this book? Because you are excited about change. You want to do things differently because you, and many others, believe we can and should deliver better learning experiences.

Let's tackle today's educational challenges with creative solutions that benefit from the countless possibilities to learn and meet the ever-changing needs of our learners with LXD.

I'd like to take a closer look at the developments that enable LXD to flourish and the qualities of LXD that make it an appealing alternative approach to shape the way we learn.

We love a great experience

Why do people love to travel, eat out, play games, go to the movies, and visit museums? They enjoy and appreciate having a wonderful experience.

We all love to invest our time and money in memorable experiences, not just to enjoy them in the moment but to enjoy them when we reflect on them. A great experience can last a lifetime. Just think about that amazing trip you took years ago. After all this time it still brings a smile to your face. You can still remember vivid details and revive some of the moments in your mind.

The value we put on experiences has increased over the last decades. This phenomenon is fundamental to the experience economy. We live in a new era of economic development that emphasizes the value of experiences.

There have been four economic eras in human history according to economists Joseph Pine and James Gilmore. We started as farmers in an agricultural economy. Then the industrial revolution made us factory workers in the industrial period. After time, products turned into services as we became service providers. And now, after the service economy, we are said to be living in an experience economy.

Quality of experience

In the experience economy it's all about the quality of the experience that you offer to your clients. Outstanding experiences are highly valued, and your customers are more than happy to pay a lot of money for this.

A well-known example is Starbucks (**FIGURE 2.1**). Originally coffee was a commodity. You bought a bag of coffee beans that you would grind yourself. Later someone figured out that if you grind it first and put it in a nice package, people pay more money for added convenience. Getting a cup of coffee as a service at a coffee shop is even more convenient and of course more expensive. But the smart people at Starbucks turned ordering and drinking a cup of coffee into an experience. Their interior, smell, product selection, music, and service enabled them to double or triple coffee prices.

There's a lesson to be learned here: People highly value a great experience. In fact, we love to spend our time and money on something memorable.

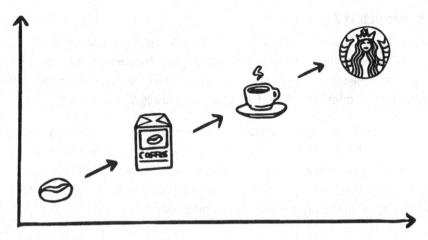

FIGURE 2.1 *From bean to brand.*

The concept of the experience economy hasn't really been embraced in the world of learning. The focus is traditionally on "What do you learn?" instead of "How is this experience going to impact the learner?" The second question is much broader than defining learning objectives. It challenges you to figure out how the learner will be challenged and impacted on a personal, academic, or professional level. The learning experience you design has the power to change people on different levels.

This is no different in learning. We've all had learning experiences that we treasure — experiences that amazed, engaged, and inspired us. As a learning experience designer, you strive to create such learning experiences.

Whenever you design a learning experience, ask yourself this question: Will the time (and money) the learner invests in this experience be worth it? It's a simple and essential question. Time is something invaluable. Unlike money, once you've taken someone's time, you can't give it back.

Once you regard other people's time as precious, your attitude will change, and with that your designs will change.

Is it worth it?

Now the big question is, what makes a learning experience worthwhile? The answer depends on many different things such as who is your design for, what are their goals, and where will it take place? It's up to learning experience designers to ask and answer these kinds of questions.

These questions go beyond "What are the learning objectives?" or "What is the goal of the client?" You want to dig deeper and discover what matters to the learner and what kind of experience will have a positive impact on their lives. These kinds of questions will be discussed in this book, and it will point you in the right direction to find answers.

Evolution of design

The role and application of design and design principles have changed dramatically in recent years. They are no longer reserved for the creative community as they have spread to different domains.

Design used to be a separate field of expertise concerned with making products that looked good and worked well. Over time the products that were designed grew in complexity. The design of an iPhone or an online shop requires different methods and skills than designing a poster or a chair. Today design is used to offer better experiences and services and solve complex problems. This has redefined the role, application, and value of design. LXD is a clear example of this development. It is a design discipline that has emerged to meet the demands of today's expectations and challenges.

Design ethics

The work of today's designers impacts our lives on many levels. It has improved how we work, communicate, re-create, socialize, and learn. Successful designs can have both upsides and downsides. For example, you can design a mobile game that millions love to play. At a glance everybody is happy. Your game makes you money, and players are enjoying themselves. But what happens when your gameplay is a bit too addictive?

Players may spend way too much time on their phones neglecting other people and responsibilities. Kids may take all their allowance or use their parents' credit card to buy in-game purchases. Every design you create is an intervention in someone's life. As a designer, you should be aware of the consequences and take responsibility.

This responsibility underlines the importance of design ethics. Under-standing the ethical aspects of your designs is vital to being a successful contemporary designer. You could say design has evolved from the aes-thetics of design to the ethics of design. A great design looks good, feels great, works well, and has a positive impact on the people you design for and the world around them. LXD fits perfectly in this evolution of design as the goal is to contribute to people's development and well-being. The impact of a well-designed learning experience goes beyond reaching a learning objective as it aims to bring about positive change in the life of the learner and the world around them. Taking on this responsibility is what many love about LXD.

Role of the designer

As design evolves, the role of the designer changes. It has become less isolated and more versatile, demanding, and challenging.

Several design disciplines have crossed over into other fields of exper-tise. For example, game designers have entered the field of healthcare. Designing a game to improve people's health requires a multidisciplinary team with designers, developers, and medical specialists. Each of them has their own perspective. The role of the designer is combining these different perspectives into a game that is fun to play and does what it is supposed to do: improve the players' health. The designer plays a central part in guiding the multidisciplinary team toward a successful outcome.

Within multidisciplinary teams, we are more inclined to think outside the box while being less protective of our own field of expertise. This open-minded attitude is also necessary for being a learning experience designer. In essence, LXD is a crossover from the field of design into the world of learning. Being open to other perspectives and feeling comfortable in a multidisciplinary environment makes you a better learning experience designer. Having different types of designers crossing over into other areas of expertise has helped to pave the way for LXD.

Technological innovation

Advancement in technology has a huge impact on our daily lives. In our professional lives we've come to depend on the speed and convenience of online communication and collaboration.

The tools we use, such as smartphones, tablets, and laptops, allow us to move around and do our jobs basically anywhere we like (**FIGURE 2.2**). Just imagine not being able to use online services for a month. It would be a challenge, that's for sure.

Our private lives have also changed profoundly. Our social interaction often takes place on social networks and via messenger services on our phones. We live our lives both in the real world and in the virtual world. Online videos and (mobile) games are an important source of entertainment. Basically, you could center your life around the devices you use.

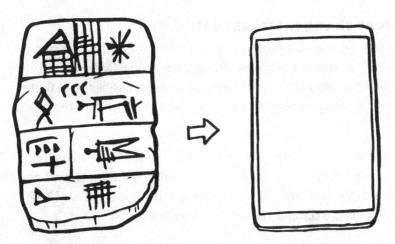

FIGURE 2.2 *Tablets then and now.*

For some reason, the impact of technology on education is limited. Yes, there is e-learning, but that's mostly for corporate learning. And when you look at the level of innovation in e-learning, it is quite limited. A lot of e-learning is similar in its design and often based on traditional instruction in a digital environment. You rarely hear people get excited over the prospect of doing an e-learning course.

As the world is changing dramatically, our schools seem to be falling behind. The adaptation of new technology is quite limited in our classrooms. Yes, you will find some laptops, iPads, and a Digi board, but the way students are educated hasn't changed much overall.

There seems to be hesitation or even fear among educators to invite new technologies into their classrooms. In fact, when I did some research about the use of computers in schools, there was a teacher who strongly resisted any form of modern technology for her students. This teacher may be an exception to the rule, but education has never been known for its progressive and innovative culture.

Don't fear change, embrace it

At the same time, there's a growing number of teachers and other learning professionals who are ready for change. They see new possibilities in new technologies, and they want to embrace these possibilities to find new ways of learning and enhance the quality of the learning experiences they offer.

More and more people want to see the way we live and work reflected in the way we learn to get students and professionals ready for today's and tomorrow's challenges. And I'm pretty sure you feel the same way. The need for change is a common reason people get into LXD.

Using an approach like LXD can help you to break free from tradition and explore new ways to teach, support, and guide learners in a relevant and contemporary way.

To be clear, LXD is not necessarily about new technology. Technology can play an important role in offering a high-quality learning experience. Obviously, you need to choose and use technology in a way that enables the learner to reach certain goals. It really doesn't matter if you are using ancient technology or state-of-the-art technology, as long as it gets the job done.

A fresh perspective

LXD offers a fresh perspective on how to shape the way we learn. It enables you to see things differently and discover new possibilities to create unique learning experiences.

Many people, like you, sense that we can do better when it comes to how we design, facilitate, and enable learning. There are a lot of changes and developments in the world of learning that offer a seemingly endless number of possibilities to (re-)design how we learn. If you want to benefit from these possibilities, you may need to change your perspective first.

What I've learned as a designer in the field of education is that I see things differently. As an outsider, you are less bound by common practices, assumptions, and traditions. This enables you to think freely and take a different approach.

A change in perspective enables you to see what else is possible when it comes to shaping the way we learn. When you think about it, we have a lot of options to choose from and even more options to design a learning experience. You want to make the right choices and pick the best options. LXD can help you with that by providing the right perspective, skills, knowledge, and methods that will structure, guide, and fuel your design process. It all starts with being able to see things in a different way, from the perspective of a designer.

The designer's perspective

Your perspective determines how you observe, what you see, how you reflect on what you see, and how you give meaning to your observations.

Designers look for shapes, patterns, details, and opportunities that others may overlook. For example, fashion designer Paul Smith is always observing the world around him, taking notes, and taking photographs. What may look like a random collection of images and words is a source of inspiration for creating a new theme for the upcoming collection of clothes.

Seeing things differently

Graphic designer Paula Scher is famous for her typography. Just like Paul Smith, she uses observation as a powerful skill to become a better designer. When Paula walks around in her hometown of New York, she sees typography everywhere. These everyday

observations feed her creativity. She gets her best ideas when she is in a taxicab just staring out the window and sketching. She says, "I'm allowing my subconscious to take over so that I can free associate."

Observation is not only a great source of inspiration for designers; it is also a critical skill when it comes to creating your designs. When you are working on a design, such as a logo, a poster, a sweater, or a chair, you are continuously making design choices based on your own observations.

By looking at and analyzing the design in each step of the creative process, you decide what works and what doesn't. The ability to look at and reflect on your own work in order to improve it is a rich tradition in both design and arts. In essence, a modern designer is using the same skills as a Renaissance painter. Back when I was studying graphic design, I had art classes, which is where I discovered the importance of observation. Later when I studied interaction design, I learned to value observation in a completely different way.

Just like musicians hear things differently, a designer sees things differently. The visual component is a big part of almost any design discipline and developing an eye for design is part of being a designer.

Focus of a designer

The work of a designer is to be experienced by people. It's these people who you focus on and design for. Having your focus on the people who eventually decide if your design actually works comes natural to designers.

Your goal as a designer is to understand who they are, empathize with their goals, and involve them in the design process. This concept is called *human-centered design*. When you apply human-centered design to learning, something special happens: You shift your focus in fundamental ways.

Traditionally in education the teacher is the focus of attention in creating learning products. The teacher is provided with materials and teaching aids that support teaching. The teacher is the expert trying to transfer knowledge to the students. This is what struck me when I started working with educational publishers. Their business model is to get schools and teachers on board. Simply put, they are the ones buying their school-books, so they are the ones they focus on.

The focus of a learning experience designer is always on the learner. You shift your focus from the teacher to the learner. At the same time, you shift your focus from teaching to learning. I know this sounds obvious, but you would be surprised to see how many educational professionals struggle with this change in focus. And while it may seem like a small change, the consequences are quite dramatic.

I know many learning professionals who are expected not to focus on the learner but on the needs of their clients.

A different method

How does a designer work? And why is that relevant to designing better learning experiences? It is all about creating new possibilities to learn by using the creative process.

The field of learning is rooted in (applied) educational science. While there are various titles for educational professionals in different parts of the world, there are clear similarities when it comes to the methods they apply. In general, it is a highly structured, methodical, and analytical approach focused on efficient learning. This systematic approach works really well for selecting and combining the right solutions that are proven to work.

The approach of a learning experience designer is fundamentally differ-ent. LXD is a design discipline that is rooted in (applied) art. Just like other design disciplines, its methods are highly creative, iterative, and often experimental. This is ideal if you want to try things that haven't been done before and create new possibilities to learn. When I look at the type of clients I serve, they generally come to me when standard solutions fall short and they need a unique design to reach their goals.

The LXD process is a process of creation. While this process is struc-tured, it leaves a lot of space to move around and is never predictable. At the beginning of a design process the end result is not yet defined. The design takes shape over time through several iterations.

This process is fueled by the creativity of the designer and revolves around the people they design for, the learners. By listening to their sto-ries and observing their actions, a designer is able to empathize with the learner and discover new possibilities to solve their problems, tackle their challenges, or address their needs.

A designer is not afraid to break new ground, looking for and experiment-ing with new possibilities and things that may be overlooked by others.

This enables you to create original, elegant, and effective solutions to the problems you need to solve.

Where others may choose the best solution out of a number of existing options, a designer creates new options to choose from in searching for the best possible solution. This offers a level of creative freedom that people love as they are free to explore new types of learning experiences. Nothing is set in stone; anything is possible!

Later in this book we will dig deeper into the design process and discuss how to design a learning experience.

Better results

The primary reason people get excited about LXD is the sense that it can help them create better learning experiences that lead to better results. When applied the right way, LXD can really make a difference in the lives of the learners.

When we talk about better results, we must start by asking: what is a good result for a learner? Traditionally, a good result means completing a course, passing a test, or getting a high grade. Of course, you want the learner to do well and score high on assessment, but you should aim for more. It's not just about what grades you get but about how you get to those grades. It's about the journey and the destination.

Let's say you redesign a course. What if the learners achieve identical grades or scores but have a far more enjoyable and engaging learning experience? Would that be a better outcome? I think so!

From the many teachers that I've trained, I've seen that their students value the experience more when the teachers put in the effort to redesign (parts of) their course using LXD principles. Often the quantifiable results are better, the students get higher grades, but when those results are similar, the teachers and students are still excited.

The students enjoyed a different kind of experience than the ones they are used to, and the teacher had fun redesigning the course. Also, the teachers learned a lot from putting their design into action. Their design was put to the test, and they gained valuable insights.

When they iterate their design once or twice, they will probably see the grades go up as well, if they haven't already. It's a process of trial and error. I can assure you that any learner appreciates the time and effort you put into providing them with a better learning experience. In fact, I've received specific feedback from learners that they felt a design was made specifically for them, which they truly appreciated and which improved their performance.

Is the approach of a learning experience designer better than any other approach? Not necessarily. Some situations require a different approach. It all depends on various variables such as the expectations of the client, the type of learner and the environment you design for, and the engagement of the different stakeholders.

I've redesigned several courses that led to better results in terms of the engagement, satisfaction, and performance of the learner. The original designs were solid but a bit traditional and focused on providing accessible content in a clearly structured way. My designs were focused on providing a meaningful experience with rich interaction, engaging stories, and appealing visualizations. Learner feedback pointed out how they appreciated the attention that was given to the design as they enjoyed it and were eager to learn (more). They felt engaged, motivated, and challenged in unexpected, interesting, and fun ways.

In conclusion, the quality of the *experience* matters, and that's where LXD shines.

A better experience leads to better results.

Creating a great learning experience is a pleasure for the learner and for the designer. That's what makes my job so easy to love.

Why LXD matters

I've observed a desire and need to approach things differently when it comes to shaping the way we learn.

What excites people about LXD is it enables them to create the kind of learning experiences that fulfill the needs of today's learner. Let's review the elements of why focusing on experience matters for learning.

We all love *a great experience*. Whether it is a vacation, a night on the town, dinner with friends, or a day of shopping, we are looking and paying for experiences that are memorable. Great learning experiences shouldn't be any different. People have come to expect more, and LXD can provide them with high-quality experiences to learn from.

Designers creating learning experiences is a perfect example of the *evolution of design*. Design has evolved from making things that look good and work well to solving complex problems in creative ways. You see designers crossing over into other fields such as healthcare, sports, and education. As such, the role of designers has become more versatile and challenging. A broader application of design is also illustrated by the popularity of design thinking. This has contributed to a broader acceptance of design in companies, schools, and other organizations.

When you solve complex problems, such as educational challenges, you need the right technology to do the job. Ongoing *technological innovation* provides us with an endless variety to facilitate learning. If you want to benefit from these options, you need to choose and use technology wisely. LXD helps you to make choices that work for the learner and fit the circumstances you design for.

LXD offers *a fresh perspective* on learning that enables you to see things differently. That's the first step to mastering LXD. Once you see things in a different way, you can start doing things in a different way. That's when you need *a different method* to reach your goals.

Using design methods can lead to surprising and exciting outcomes, which is helpful when it comes to creating meaningful learning experiences. Learning experience designers are known for doing things that haven't been done before. That's the essence of a creative process, to create something unique. Providing learning with unique experiences reinforces that not all learners are the same and that you can respect these differences in your design.

You can imagine that if you see things differently and do things differently, you will get different results. Is different better? Not always, but often you will get *better results* that go beyond reaching learning objectives and have a positive impact on the lives of learners.

IF WE WANT TO CHANGE
THE WAY WE LEARN

WE HAVE TO LEARN
HOW TO CHANGE

IF WE WANT TO CHANGE
THE WAY WE LEARN

WE HAVE TO LEARN
HOW TO CHANGE

Nine rules of learning experience design

TO KEEP IN MIND

These rules apply to the design of any learning experience and will help shift or broaden your perspective on how we can shape the way we learn.

Rules? That's a strong word. Generally, designers are known for bending or breaking rules to produce groundbreaking designs. I chose the word because I feel strongly about these key principles, which are foundational to my practice. You'll find they don't limit your creativity, and each rule builds upon the other rules.

I want to introduce these rules before we go into designing a learning experience in the next chapter and so we can refer to them throughout the book.

1. We learn from experience.

2. Every experience is unique.

3. Learning is a continuous, dynamic, and holistic process.

4. How we learn is influenced by emotion.

5. Learning is focused on both process and outcome.

6. Learning experience design is human-centered.

7. More senses makes more sense.

8. (Inter)active is effective.

9. Learning experiences should be positive, personal, and profound.

RULE 1: *We learn from experience*

There are many theories about how we learn. There are specific theories such as how toddlers develop language skills or how students learn mathematical formulas. There are also more general theories such as the benefits of chunking information to increase retention or how long it generally takes before we forget knowledge we don't apply.

When you think about how we learn, there is one principle that applies to any situation. It's a principle that is so fundamental that you might even not be aware of it:

Everything we learn comes from experience.

Our lives are a collection of experiences. Many are ordinary, everyday experiences such as brushing your teeth, buying groceries, or parking your car. Some experiences can be unforgettable, extraordinary experiences such as your first kiss or traveling to your dream destination.

All these experiences combined determine who you are, how you see the world around you, what you think, and what you do. We are shaped through our past experiences and transformed by future experiences.

Don't limit yourself

Sometimes we are inclined to have a rather limited perception of what a learning experience should or could be like. In education I've seen many examples of people who expect learning to take place in a certain way, for example through classroom instruction or lectures. Also, e-learning professionals can be restricted in their views, which are often influenced by the technology they use. The result is that e-learning modules often use the same predictable format, are made with the same tools, and have a similar look and feel even though they are created for different people with different goals.

YOU CANNOT LEARN WITHOUT EXPERIENCE

YOU CANNOT
EXPERIENCE
WITHOUT LEARNING

NF

LXD aims to provide learners with experiences that are unique to them and their needs. I've never designed two similar learning experiences because I believe no two people or situations are the same.

Endless possibilities

Being aware that we learn from what we experience opens up a world of possibilities. Think about the incredible variety in types of experiences you have had in your lifetime. If there are so many kinds of experiences to be had, there are just as many ways to learn.

The main goal of this first rule is to make you aware of what's possible. An experience doesn't have to be limited because we have preconceived notions of what a learning experience should be like. Enjoy your freedom!

RULE 2: *Every experience is unique (and so are you)*

There are two reasons why every experience you have is unique:

- Your own previous experiences

- Your personal characteristics

Into every experience each person brings their own unique set of previous experiences. Just think of how many different experiences you've had over the course of your lifetime. This collection of experiences makes up your past and your memories. At the same time, it influences your present and future. Obviously, people with different pasts will experience new experiences differently.

When you think about it, it is simply impossible to share a perfectly identical experience. In other words, each experience is unique. This is also what makes you unique. You are the owner of a unique set of personal experiences that have made you who you are today.

Each individual constructs their own experience based on personal characteristics. Remember how, as a kid, everything seemed bigger since you were smaller. This is just one example of how our physical, mental, and emotional characteristics play a role in how we actually experience things.

The concept of adaptive learning experiences really makes sense when you take this uniqueness into account. Adaptivity means that not everybody has an identical experience. For example, a learner can be offered different options to choose from on how to proceed. Depending on their level of experience and personal preference, they can pick an option that works best for them. I've applied this in a project for teens in varying school levels. We designed different exercises with a similar goal to support the students most effectively. This is just one small example that already made a big difference. We added more adaptivity, which allowed students to take ownership of their learning journey and use their strengths to overcome their weak spots.

So, try to see if and how you can provide a more personal learning path for individual learners. This can be complicated, but it doesn't have to be.

A learning experience doesn't have to be unique like a high-tech, outrageous, or never-been-done-before experience. This is a common misconception about LXD — the idea that LXD is solely for creating extraordinary innovative experiences.

I've designed everything from simple, low-tech experiences to complex high-tech experiences. What makes these experiences unique are the original ideas, creative solutions, and sophisticated designs that you come up with. You don't have to turn an experience into a spectacle to make it unique.

You could say it's a different kind of unique.

RULE 3: *Learning is continuous, dynamic, and holistic*

Learning doesn't just happen in school or during a day of training. You can learn anywhere, anytime, and in any way because learning is a continuous, dynamic, and holistic process.

Let's look at what each of these words mean in the context of a learning experience.

Continuous

You learn all the time, whether you are aware of it or not. When you are awake, you're learning as you experience events throughout the day. In fact, even when we sleep, we are learning while the mind is processing the day's events.

We know learning doesn't begin with school, nor does it stop only when we cease actively studying. Learning continues; we can't turn it off. We can make an effort to deliberately learn something but we can't not learn. That's one of the reasons why it's good to take a break and let the things we've just learned sink in. It gives us the time to process and reflect.

Learning is not only a conscious effort. It is human nature. It is the way our brains and bodies work. We are basically programmed to learn; let's not forget this.

Dynamic

As we learn, there are many factors that impact our experience. This makes learning a dynamic process where things change all the time. First, as we learn new things, we change, sometimes in a small way and sometimes in a big way. There can be other internal changing factors like mood or level of attention and focus.

External factors such as ambient noise, temperature, and the people who surround you also impact a learning experience. Change is basically constant.

The dynamic character of learning is easily forgotten as education, e-learning, and training are often standardized to be as manageable and predictable as possible. That's great for teachers and trainers but not so much for learners.

Holistic

People are more than a set of brains. We have bodies, emotions, character traits, beliefs, and doubts. This is what makes us human.

Yet we often focus on the cognitive development by only transferring knowledge. A holistic approach is to see people as humans and not learning machines meant to process educational content. Remember the second rule: we are unique individuals who each experiences things in our own way.

A holistic approach also applies to the human experience. An experience consists of many different parts such as people, resources, activities, and spaces. You should take the complete human experience into account. A learning experience should be more than the sum of its parts.

RULE 4: *Learning is influenced by emotion*

Let's say you are designing a learning experience. You're probably thinking about what the learner will learn from this experience. Now think about this question:

How will this experience make the learner feel?

When we talk about our daily experiences, we use emotions and emotional comments to share our stories. What actually happens in those stories is often secondary to how they made us feel.

Learning is a wonderful process that can be fulfilling and rewarding. It can make us feel triumphant, confident, aware, amazed, excited, and inspired. Breaking through personal boundaries, broadening your horizon, and deepening our understanding of the world around us is what makes us feel good about learning and ourselves. We should use these emotions to benefit the learner and achieve greater results.

Unfortunately, there are also quite a few negative emotions linked to learning: back-to-school anxiety, fear of failure, bullying, frustration, peer pressure, boredom, and performance pressure, to name a few. This can bring back high school memories, but these emotions also occur in adult education.

Learners of any age can feel nervous, afraid, anxious, frustrated, sad, stressed, or helpless. These negative emotions distort and negatively impact learning experiences. That's why we need to deal with these emotions in a way that they don't undermine the learners' personal development. Instead, the emotions should strengthen the experience: on the one hand, by stimulating positive emotions such as enthusiasm, confidence, pride, gratitude, and amusement; on the other hand, by handling negative emotions respectfully and providing sufficient support.

How we feel influences how we learn. It colors our experiences — you'll want to be aware of this in your designs. Taking people's emotions into account is a vital part of human-centered design.

Understanding what the learner might feel before, during, and after a learning experience is important for the design of a successful learning experience. This requires empathy for the learner when you do your research and when you create and implement your design.

RULE 5: *Learning is about process and outcome*

Traditionally there has been a focus on the outcome of learning in education: specifically, a quantifiable outcome that is easy to grade and use as a basis for comparison.

Two students take a test. One scores high, and the other scores just above average. Which one did a better job? You'd assume the student with the highest score. But here's the catch. The student who scored less may have learned more. It all depends on what you look at.

Looking at the way both students have developed over time reveals how much they learned. If you start at a high level and just maintain that level, you didn't learn much. If you start at a lower level and get up to a higher level, you've learned a lot.

That's why I believe learning is about the whole learning journey, which encompasses the process and the outcome. Unfortunately, there can be an unhealthy focus on the outcome alone, specifically, on measuring the outcome. This distorts the process of learning as learners are more interested in passing a test than learning something new. I believe there are two things that can positively impact the learner in this regard. First, we should value both the process and the outcome. Just look at the difference between how learners enter an experience and how they leave.

Second, we should redefine learning outcomes. This will be discussed in more detail later in the book; for now I'd like to point out that a learning outcome should be meaningful and valuable to the learner.

An experience is not a snapshot of a moment in time. It's more like a movie that takes place over time. Assessing learners based on a snapshot isn't fair. It doesn't do justice to their personal experience. As a designer, I'm not interested in taking snapshots. I've seen how a great process leads to a great outcome. It's not one or the other; it's the combination that can make a real difference for the learner.

RULE 6: *Learning experience design is human-centered*

Human-centered design is a design principle that is at the core of several design disciplines such as interaction design, user experience design, and, of course, LXD.

Care for the people you design for

When I ask teachers what they love about their job, nine out of ten times I get this answer: *I love my students*. They care about their students, and they want the best for them. By giving students the attention and the assistance they need, their students grow as learners and as people. This is what drives the quality of education more than anything else in my opinion.

LXD is no different. You care for the people you design for. It's the only way to design an experience that connects with the learner both on a cognitive and emotional level. It requires a personal experience that enables the learner to flourish. And there is only one way to achieve that: human-centered design.

Put the learner at the heart of your design and your design process

When you want to design in a human-centered way, you have to put the learner at the heart of your design and your design process. This means you have to involve the people who will be part of the experience in the actual design process. This can be done through research, testing, and co-creation.

Remember, we don't design for companies, schools, or any other organization. We put the people first, and the rest is secondary.

We design for people.

It's easy to fall back on old habits of focusing on our own expertise and the content or goals we consider to be important. It happens to us all, myself included. That's why I remind myself from time to time that we are not nearly as important as the learner.

RULE 7: *More senses makes more sense*

Let's say you want to teach a non-English speaker the word *apple*. You have two options to choose from. Either you use a picture of an apple or a real apple. What would you pick?

A real apple, of course. Our brain is wired in a way that makes it easier to remember and learn things that stimulate more senses. A multisensory sensation leads multiple sources of information through our senses into our brain.

The brain can easily process these streams of information as they are all part of a bigger picture. The shape, the taste, and the smell of the apple offer a more complete and natural experience.

If you look at the memory structure of our brains, it consists of three parts:

- Sensory memory
- Working memory
- Long-term memory

How we process, store, and retrieve information depends on how these parts operate.

Let's get back to the example of learning the word *apple*. In this illustration I've visualized how your brain processes a real apple:

When you take a bite, you see, hear, touch, taste, and smell the apple. Every sense sends a separate signal to your working memory. Compared to watching the image of an apple, where you only see an apple, the stream of information is much richer and more natural to process for your working memory. As a result, it can trigger memories from your long-term memory, like eating your grandmother's delicious apple pie when you were a child. Engaging all the senses makes experiences easier to remember. In other words, using more senses makes more sense.

RULE 8: *(Inter)active is effective*

Would you like to design a passive learning experience? Probably not. Passive experiences don't sound very appealing or inspiring.

Yet we are quite used to passive learning experiences where sitting still and listening is all we do. While there is nothing wrong with listening to a good story, there are many ways to make an experience more engaging.

Keeping learners active by offering different types of activities can help to get and keep them motivated. It makes the experience more versatile and less predictable. It increases the energy level and the excitement to learn.

In schools, students often look more alive during breaks. They are free to move around, socialize, eat a bit, and do what they prefer. There's a valuable lesson to be learned here.

A great example is playing applied games. Games can keep the players focused and entertained. A bit of competition or collaboration can push them to a next level. There's a chance of winning, and the process of playing is fun. These are ideal aspects of games that can be used for learning.

Being physically active is also great for learning. In general, physical activity has proved to contribute to a healthy brain.

Adding interactivity can do wonders for the learner. Being able to influence the path you take is empowering. It is likely to increase engagement during the learning experience and commitment to the learning outcome.

If you have a level of influence over the path and outcome of the experience, you're likely to be more engaged and committed to the outcome. Being an active participant instead of a passive observer isn't just more enjoyable; it makes the experience more relevant and personal.

RULE 9: *Learning experiences should be positive, personal, and profound*

What makes a great learning experience? That's an important question for LX designers.

As an LXD teacher and trainer, I've asked many students and professionals to share the best learning experience they had. The examples they shared are wildly varied. No two experiences are identical. It made me wonder, what do all these different experiences have in common? What are the magical ingredients that make these experiences great? My conclusion is that every learning experience should be positive, personal, and profound.

Positive

How do you make somebody want to learn? You need to offer an experience that is appealing and inviting to start learning. This is a critical first step for the success of any learning experience. Once they get started, it should motivate them to keep learning. Finding out what is appealing for a learner helps you, as a designer, tailor the experience to a learner's personal preferences.

"What will I get out of this experience?"

That's an important question for you to answer. A learning experience must be rewarding and offer a positive result, something they gain from their effort. That's obvious. However, it's not so simple to define the desired learning outcome.

Defining the learning outcome is a good way to start the design of a learning experience. It makes you focus on the learner and what's in it for them.

On an emotional level, a learning experience should also be enjoyable and give a positive feeling. It should be something they can reflect on with a smile. This doesn't mean the experience has to be all fun and laughs. People enjoy different types of experiences for different reasons. So, try to figure out what would give your learners a positive feeling for an enjoyable learning experience.

Personal

Learning is a human and preferably social process. Therefore, the design of a learning experience should be human-centered. This means that you use the characteristics, qualities, wants, and needs of the learners and teachers as the foundation of your design. In my opinion, learning isn't about the medium you choose; it's about people.

Every individual brings a set of personal previous experiences into a new learning experience. This ultimately affects both the learning experience itself and the outcome of the learning experience. We should offer unique experiences for unique individuals by making them adaptive to the personal needs and characteristics of the individual learner.

People want to be taken seriously. They want to learn about real things. What makes an experience real?

Authenticity.

An authentic experience resonates with the learner because it's real and honest. It's the opposite of fake and superficial.

Profound

What is the difference between information and knowledge? Meaning. What we learn gives meaning to who we are and what we do. To convey knowledge, a learning experience must be meaningful. If there's no real meaning to what we learn, there's basically no point in learning it at all.

Finding meaning in what you learn is a magical thing that makes you want to learn more.

If it's too easy, it's no fun.

Learning needs to be challenging; without challenge, you don't learn. Challenge makes learning fun. Overcoming obstacles and learning from failure can both be powerful learning experiences. You see this in games where the right amount of challenge makes a player want to keep going until the end of the game. You want a learner to do the same and feel good about how they persevered and what they have achieved.

Finally, everybody has that one great teacher that they will always remember. Their teaching had an impact on their lives. For a learning experience to be lasting, it needs to have an impact on the learner. You need to really connect on different levels, not only mentally but also emotionally and, if possible, physically or spiritually.

*Nothing ever becomes real
till it is experienced.*

— JOHN KEATS, POET

Chapter 3

What is *GOOD* learning experience design?

Learning experience design (LXD) is the process of creating learning experiences that enable the learner to achieve the desired learning outcome in a human-centered and goal-oriented way.

Defining learning experience design

LXD offers a new way to explore and create experiences that people learn from. In essence, it's about using design skills to figure out what experience would work best for a person or group of people in a specific situation.

To get a better understanding of what LXD is, we will break it down into smaller parts in this section: experience, design, and learning (**FIGURE 3.1**). These terms on their own are self-explanatory, but together they tell a lot about what LXD really is, including being both human-centered and goal-oriented.

After that, we will dig deeper into the origins of LXD and explore a conceptual framework to define the field of LXD and its interdisciplinary nature using four quadrants.

We will also examine how LXD differs from (or is similar to) related disciplines. Finally, we'll look at the qualities of a learning experience designer and the path to living comfortably in the four quadrants.

FIGURE 3.1 *Learning + experience + design = LXD.*

Experience

Everything we learn comes from experience, that's a fact. So, if we learn from what we experience, why not design learning as an experience?

What is an experience? Often, we refer to experiences as things that are memorable due to their spectacular, extraordinary, or unexpected nature like riding a roller coaster, traveling the world, or running into a celebrity. While these are all experiences, they are not the only experiences we have. In fact, most of our experiences are anything but extraordinary. They are what happen to us in everyday life like commuting to work, having dinner, or getting the kids to bed.

> *An experience is any situation you encounter that takes an amount of time and leaves an impression.*

Experience is basically everything that happens to you from the moment you wake up to the moment you fall asleep.

Of course, not every experience is particularly educational. Some experiences can be straight-out boring and best forgotten. Fortunately, we've all had experiences that teach us lessons that benefit us for the rest of our lives. It's these kinds of experiences, whether they are designed, completely spontaneous, or somewhere in between, that we aim to design as learning experience designers.

Design

LXD is a creative design discipline. You use the designer's perspective, skills, methods, and tools to create memorable and meaningful experiences.

As designers, we create things with a specific target audience, market, or demographic in mind. Our work comes in many shapes and sizes and serves a need, desire, or purpose for those people. Examples are a website for a user, a poster for a spectator, a game for a player, an infographic for a reader, or an experience for a learner. Understanding the people you design for through analysis and empathy allows you to come up with original ideas and elegant designs that people enjoy and appreciate. This requires a mix of creative and analytical skills and an approach that allows for new and exciting solutions to emerge.

Having a design process that allows creativity to flourish is essential. Working with an iterative, flexible creative process, where the outcome is not predictable, is the backbone of LXD. It enables you to experiment and try new things. At the same time, it helps you to focus your creativity and structure your efforts toward creating something that works on all levels.

Learning

LXD is about learning and not so much about teaching, instructions, education, or training. We focus on the learner and their experience.

There are endless ways to learn. It can be a conscious effort or take place without even being aware of it. Learning doesn't just happen once you sit down and open this book, and it doesn't stop when you close this book. You learn so much more as you make the things your own through active processing, reflection, and application.

If you want to learn something, your senses need to be active. When your senses are active, you are experiencing. That's why you cannot learn without experience.

Furthermore, when you experience something, *you are learning*. It's the way humans operate. With every experience, your brain is:

- Strengthening existing neural connections
- Adding new neural connections
- Changing existing neural connections

This means that the structures in your brain are changed, however so slightly, by each new experience. This illustrates how you cannot experience without learning.

There are countless theories on learning and strategies to apply to them. Which ones you need depends on the type of experience you design. Fundamental to LXD is an understanding of how people learn from experience. This is a big topic, but we'll begin an exploration in Chapter 4, "Experiential Learning."

As stated, you want to design a learning experience that enables the learner to reach the desired learning outcome. How do you do that? By using your design skills and making the experience human-centered and goal-oriented.

Human centered

Learning is a human and preferably social process. Putting the people at the center of your design process is called **human-centered design.**

This is an important part of how and why LXD works. It means you have to:

- Get to know the learners, the people you design for

- Be able to empathize with them as learners

You want to figure out what drives them and how you can ignite their intrinsic motivation. That's why getting in touch with your target audience through interviews and observations (user research) is indispensable. Beyond this, involving learners in co-creation can provide key insights.

People are both rational and emotional beings. We all have wants, needs, hopes, fears, and doubts. A great learning experience has to connect on a personal level. Being able to distinguish and act upon differences between groups of learners, and even individual learners, is key.

For this part to succeed, not only do you have to know your target audience, but you need to understand how people learn from experience. Consulting or working with neuroscientists, cognitive psychologists, or other learning experts is highly recommended.

Goal oriented

A learning experience will make no sense if you don't reach your goals. Choosing and formulating the right goals is an important part of designing any learning experience.

As with most design projects, this can be quite a challenge, depending on the scale and complexity of the experience that you are designing. The first goal to understand is the project goal, generally set by the client.

Then, you must come up with activities that enable the learner to reach their specific goals in this context. This is what separates a good learning experience designer from a great one.

That's where a structured, thorough, and innovative approach can really make a difference, as you will see in Chapter 6, "The Learning Experience Canvas."

One important aspect of LXD is the form, medium, or technology you choose for a learning experience. This choice is primarily based on the goals of the learner.

Start with the end in mind so you know what you're aiming for!

Start with formulating the desired learning outcome, and every next step in the design process, including the choice of your medium or technology, is geared toward the desired learning outcome: starting with the end in mind. If you know what you are aiming for, you are more likely to get there.

The origins of learning experience design

You've just read what learning experience design is. Right now, I'll dive into the origins of LXD — where does it come from?

There are two stories to be told here: a personal story and a conceptual one. The latter is about the conceptual framework that explains how different disciplines from the fields of design and education have merged into LXD. The personal story is about my role in the creation and development of LXD, and I will share how it all began for me.

Let's go back to the beginning: to the summer of 2007. At the time I was working both as a teacher and as an interaction designer. While working in the field of education as a teacher with the perspective of a designer, I soon found out my views on education were rather different in several ways.

Being a designer, I was used to figuring out what people need in order to create a design that works for them. As a teacher, I was expected to tell the students what's important instead of asking them questions about their needs. I wanted to offer them memorable experiences and focus on their personal development instead of structuring, delivering, and assessing content.

In this setting, creating experiences in a human-centered way was extremely challenging. Any ideas had to fit into the structures of the educational system of the university. This left me with little time and space to experiment. I saw the variety of students — no two students are the same — but all were provided with very similar and rather predictable experiences. I saw a lot of room for improvement.

Being the odd one out meant I wasn't burdened with what education traditionally is supposed to be. I didn't want to let the educational system limit me, my creativity, or my desire to provide my students with the best experiences I had to offer.

That summer I asked myself a question:

How do we learn?

The answer is simple:

We learn from what we experience.

As an interaction designer, I was already designing experiences. For example, I designed user experiences that enabled people to reach their goals. So, what if I could use those skills and that process to design experiences for people to learn from? What would that be called? Exactly: learning experience design.

When I entered **learning experience design** into Google's search bar, I was shocked by the results. There were zero hits! There was literally nothing to be found about learning experience design. It simply didn't exist.

As a designer and teacher, it made perfect sense to apply my expertise as a designer to the field of learning. Why not use your creativity to offer students better experiences? There are so many ways to shape the way we learn. All these possibilities got me excited. Unfortunately, the rest of the world was less excited and didn't know, understand, or share my passion for the concept of designing learning experiences.

To be fair, when I started developing and applying LXD, it was still very much a work in progress. The outlines were there, but a lot of details were missing. Years of teaching LXD and working for clients has helped me to develop a strong foundation. When I created the Learning Experience Canvas design tool, it took on a life of its own. People from around the world started using it, and a global community was slowly but surely coming into existence. Today this vibrant community is growing rapidly.

Fields of expertise

LXD is an interdisciplinary field of expertise. It incorporates elements of different disciplines such as interaction design, neuroscience, cognitive psychology, and teaching — bringing them into a new design discipline.

In essence, LXD is a combination of two domains: design and learning (**FIGURE 3.2**).

Leaving it at this would be oversimplified as both design and learning are broad and diverse domains. That's why each domain is divided into two parts. The upper parts focus on human aspects, and the lower parts focus on achieving goals (**FIGURE 3.3**).

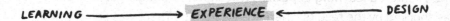

FIGURE 3.2 *The domains of design and learning come together in LXD.*

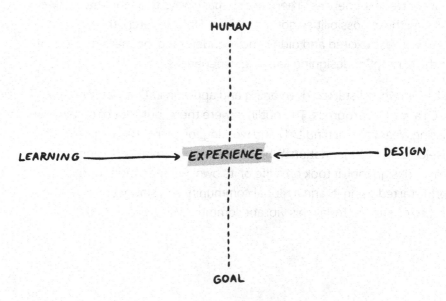

FIGURE 3.3 *The axis of human/goals is added.*

The practice of LXD is rooted in these four quadrants. On a conceptual level, each quadrant represents part of what you must do when you design a learning experience (**FIGURE 3.4**).

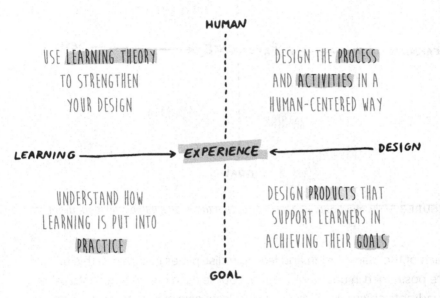

FIGURE 3.4 *Descriptions of the four quadrants from which LXD emerged.*

If one or more of these quadrants is missing, your design is going to fall apart. For example, you can use all the learning theory you want, but if the process isn't well-designed and the activities are boring, the experience is going to be terrible. Or, you might have a great product, like a game for K–12 students that takes five hours to complete. That's not practical as the students will lose concentration, and it probably won't fit in a regular school day.

Mastering each quadrant or having a team that is able to cover all aspects enables you to apply LXD successfully.

Right now, this might all sound a bit conceptual. You might wonder exactly which disciplines have shaped LXD. **FIGURE 3.5** includes these disciplines and illustrates the roots of LXD and its interdisciplinary nature.

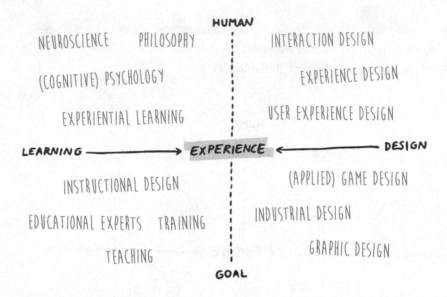

FIGURE 3.5 *The quadrants with disciplines that (generally) inhabit each quadrant.*

Each of the many design and learning disciplines included in this graphic are positioned in quadrants, but of course each one extends into other quadrants as well. Each discipline adds its own elements, and together they form the foundation of LXD. Let's explore each of these four quadrants a bit further.

The human aspects of design

The upper-right quadrant includes design disciplines that are about human experience. It's common practice for designers, such as user experience and interaction designers, to put people at the center of their designs. This human-centered approach enables you to offer an experience that people can relate to and that really works for them. What you design is the specific process people go through. You define the options they have, the choices they make, the things that they do, and how they reach the outcome they desire.

Goal-oriented design

The lower-right quadrant is about design disciplines that tend to focus on creating products that serve a clear purpose. The products we use to facilitate or enhance a learning experience should have both practical and appealing features. This is just like an industrial designer who designs products that are both functional and beautiful, or a graphic designer who finds creative ways to get a message across in a sophisticated way. Of course, this is not to say that there are not human aspects of these disciplines as well. Finding the right shape or form for a learning experience is a vital part of designing an effective learning experience.

Theory of learning

In the upper-left quadrant, you can see the more scientific disciplines that are about how people learn. It's essential that a learning experience designer comprehends how human cognition works and how we learn from experience. Combining experiential learning with neuroscientific and psychological insights is part of the foundation of any good learning experience. There is an interesting link between certain design disciplines, such as interaction design, and (cognitive) psychology. Designers often use psychological insights to better understand the people they design for and to create designs that work intuitively.

Learning put into practice

The lower-left quadrant is about the practical side of learning. This is where educational professionals, such as teachers and trainers, put the theory of learning into practice. Having both a theoretical and practical understanding of learning is essential. This understanding helps you to design goal-oriented learning experiences that work in real-world situations. Knowing the ins and outs of the environment you design for is especially important for the implementation of your designs. This is something instructional design addresses well. They are aware of the systems, structures, and forces at play in the schools and companies they design for.

What's missing here?

This list of disciplines is not all-encompassing. It does illustrate the aspects that are elemental to LXD. Within these domains there's room for more. A few other interesting fields could be anthropology, computer science, artificial intelligence, and architecture. They all add something different to the mix of LXD. The key here is to recognize the versatility of LXD and to keep an open mind toward any field that could help expand your expertise as a learning experience designer. I find it both enlightening and practical to invite experts to join my design team when we are working on designs with challenging goals and a special type of learner.

For example, we've worked on several learning experiences for children with learning disabilities. Thanks to several experts who know and understand these learners, we were able to provide an experience that connected with them on a cognitive and emotional level.

When you look at the origins of LXD, it's clear to see there is no one single discipline that can be regarded as the foundation of LXD. It's the combination of several disciplines that makes it unique and powerful.

Why is it important to distinguish LXD from other fields?

The ability to distinguish LXD is essential for you as a learning experience designer and for the future of LXD.

How people initially approach LXD tends to depend on their own professional background. In general, people relate LXD to the field they are familiar with. This is understandable, especially when there appear to be close similarities between LXD and their discipline. I use the word *appear* intentionally because things are not always what they seem to be. On the surface, LXD might look like several other fields, but when you dig deeper, you will uncover fundamental differences.

It is not desirable for a single professional perspective to be dominant in the definition of LXD, as it can limit the scope and depth of the field. Here are three examples I come across frequently:

- **Instructional designers** tend to see LXD as an evolution or form of instructional design.

- **User experience designers** tend to see LXD as user experience design for learners.

- **Teachers** tend to see LXD as design thinking for education.

I could easily add more examples (LXD as a subdomain of experience design or LXD as a form of service design), but you get the idea.

Looking at these three common examples, you can see how they can't all be right. Think about the kind of education you need to become a teacher, user experience designer, or instructional designer. Consider the skillset you need for each of these professions and the kinds of organizations you work in and what you deliver.

These are three fundamentally different fields, and none of them can claim to be identical to, or the sole origin of, LXD. We've seen that a wide variety of fields contributed to the birth of LXD. Choosing one or two fields as the core of LXD doesn't do justice to the interdisciplinary charac ter of LXD and the particular skillset it requires to be an effective learning experience designer.

You might wonder why this even matters. Why look at specific similarities and differences between LXD and instructional design or user experience design or design thinking? Having the ability to distinguish LXD in specific ways is essential to:

- Provide clarity

- Value each field for what it is

- Learn from other fields

- Secure the future of LXD

Provide clarity

The term *LXD* is used by different people in different ways. For example, you might see a job posting for a learning experience designer that asks for a degree in instructional design (ID) instead of asking for a design background. Most likely, they are looking for an instructional designer but using the term *learning experience designer.* Maybe it sounds more appealing, or maybe it's a lack of understanding. Either way, these kinds of misunderstandings create two problems. One is that the job applicant is misled. Two is that this can be seen as an assertion that LXD and ID are the same, which is not the case.

It is important that there be widespread clarity about what LXD is and what it isn't. That is the only way we can have meaningful discussions about the field of LXD, especially in relation to other fields.

Value each field for what it is

Each field of expertise has unique characteristics that offer value to clients, users, students, employees, and other stakeholders. This value is created by the specific perspective, skills, methods, and tools of the professional. For example, a user experience designer will bring an understanding of design research. At the same time, there are limitations to each field. If you're looking for scientific proof, design research may not be your primary need.

Knowing and understanding the qualities and the limitations of different fields enables you to value each field for what it is. This isn't to put any field down or claim superiority over other fields. It is about doing justice to the great work that is done in different fields.

Learn from other fields

Once you're able to separate one field from the other, professionals can start to learn from each other. This is my main advice to anyone entering the field of LXD from a related field: learn from each other!

The fact that people have different backgrounds offers a great opportunity to learn. We all come into the field of LXD from different directions, and each direction brings a different perspective. Practitioners with a design background can learn from people with a learning background, and vice versa.

Secure the future of LXD

This is a vital point for me personally. I've spent many years applying, developing, and promoting LXD. The growing acceptance and appreciation of LXD has led to various definitions of LXD coming from various sources. This has created a level of confusion that makes it hard for learning experience designers to clearly state their case.

> *"If there's nothing different or new about LXD,*
> *why hire a learning experience designer?"*

I've heard from multiple learning experience designers in different parts of the world, and they report hearing these kinds of remarks. Perhaps you are experiencing the same problem. Your challenge is to get your message across when there are those who don't get it or don't want to get it. Use the insights from this book — and this chapter in particular — to strengthen your story and convince people of the value and uniqueness of LXD.

Today LXD can easily be overshadowed by other, better-known fields. In the United States, instructional design is the dominant field. This creates an environment where LXD could be considered "just another name for ID." LXD could dissolve into instructional design and lose many of its unique properties.

As an emerging field that doesn't yet have the history of more established fields, we are fighting an uphill battle. Fortunately, the global LXD community is growing, and more people now have a basic understanding of what it has to offer.

More and more professionals have experienced the impact of LXD, seen the difference, and become passionate advocates. That's important because the future of LXD will be secured only when a majority of us can clearly distinguish LXD from other fields. We also need to be able to articulate these distinctions to our colleagues and clients. Only then can we value LXD for what it is and take it seriously as a field of its own.

We've established *why* it's important to distinguish LXD from closely associated disciplines or approaches. Now it's time to dive into specific similarities and differences. We'll look at instructional design, user experience design (UXD), and design thinking.

Before we get into that, I want to emphasize that this is in no way a competition. One discipline isn't better than the other. Each approach has its upsides and downsides. These comparisons are made only to clarify the differences and not to argue that one is best.

LXD and instructional design

The one field that LXD is compared to the most is instructional design.

On the surface, the two fields might appear to be similar. When you dig deeper, however, they are different in a few fundamental ways.

Did you know the field of instructional design is lesser known in Europe than it is in the United States? I was already applying and teaching LXD when I first heard about it. As I learned more about ID, it became clear to me that there are big differences between the perspectives, skills, methods, tools, and results of learning experience design and instructional design. I will explain some major differences one by one.

Perspective

A great way to explain the general difference between LXD and ID is by comparing a scientist to an artist. ID has a more scientific perspective as an applied science, while LXD has a more creative perspective as an applied art. Imagine how a scientist and an artist would separately try to solve the same problem. Their approaches and their solutions would be totally different. Both have value, and one is not necessarily better than the other. The same applies to ID and LXD. Applied science and applied art are both valid approaches with different qualities and limitations.

SCIENCE   ART

ID comes from the field of education and is intended to be used in the field of learning, generally within fairly large institutions. Emphasis is placed on measurable results. This makes sense. I know several great instructional designers who studied ID at university and who now work as instructional designers at universities.

LXD comes from the field of design, which is most often practiced by independent professionals or small firms. In all disciplines of design, a high value is placed on creativity and looking at a problem in a new way.

Being a creative professional who has taught at universities for years, I've always felt like an outsider. Being an outsider can be difficult, but it also offers a certain freedom because you tend to see and do things differently. You are not part of the system. That's one of the reasons why LXD is appealing. It offers a fresh perspective that comes from outside of the world of learning.

Skills

Imagine a typical creative professional like a graphic designer. What are the skills of this type of designer? They include having a sharp eye, empathizing with the target audience, generating original ideas, sketching visualizations to clarify and conceptualize these ideas, creating and iterating different designs, and crafting elegant and surprising ways to communicate a message. These are all essential qualities for a learning experience designer as well. They can be applied to present learners with an experience that is just as elegant, refreshing, and surprising as the work of a graphic designer. The roots of LXD lie firmly in creative design disciplines.

Instructional design has its roots in the field of learning. Learning and educational professionals come from different backgrounds and professional cultures. They have key skills such as developing content and designing curricula that fit perfectly within the academic and corporate educational systems. They also design standardized e-learning courses effectively. This requires more analytical, methodical, and scientific skills rather than artistic skills. As the name *instructional design* suggests, instruction plays an important role. This dates back to the origin of ID in the army, where clear instruction was vital. These instructional principles enable teachers, trainers, and instructors to do their jobs and provide learners with clarity and structure.

Methods

Instructional design emphasizes a methodical approach to design. According to the Association for Talent Development (ATD) website, an instructional designer applies a "systematic methodology (rooted in instructional theories and models.)"* It works with a clearly structured step-by-step process, which is often linear. Each step builds on the next and guides you toward creating a solid, well-founded design.

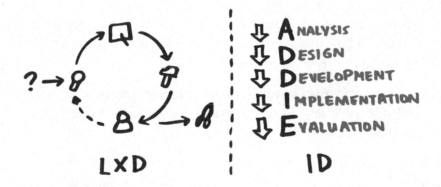

While the LXD process is also structured, it does provide more space in its process to be creative and quickly come up with different ideas, designs, and prototypes, which can be improved through iteration. There is a

*See the entry for instructional designer at www.td.org/glossary-terms.

level of unpredictability that designers love. You're not predetermining what the end result is going to be. The creative and experimental process inspires and guides you toward finding the right shape or form, like a sculptor turning a piece of stone into a sculpture or a painter turning a blank canvas into a painting.

Of course, both instructional designers and learning experience designers go through the same general steps of research, design, development, testing, and implementation. At a glance, the process in ID and LXD might look similar. However, the exact steps, how you proceed, and what you focus on during the process are not the same.

For example, an important part of LXD is prototyping your design, testing it, and improving the design through different iterations. This allows you to try new things and turn original ideas into reality. This experimental approach is vital if you want to create unique designs.

A well-known instructional design process is ADDIE, which stands for Analysis, Design, Development, Implementation, and Evaluation. It's a systematic approach that focuses on the effectiveness of learning and traditionally isn't used iteratively. ADDIE works great if each step is done thoroughly and the design is worked out in detail before you start developing. However, it leaves little space for experimentation.

In general, the instructional design process requires an analytical mindset with a scientific approach. This enables you to find and select great options that enable learners to reach their goals.

Learning experience designers have a creative mindset with a design approach. This enables them to go beyond existing options and create completely new ways to help learners reach their goals. The process supports you in your journey to a new solution and enables learning experience designers to design learning experiences that haven't been made before.

Tools

There are many tools you can use to create a learning experience. I often see learning management systems, e-learning authoring software, office software, and web services used in instructional design projects. Learning experience designers are more likely to use design tools that enable them to make more tailored designs such as Adobe software, custom apps, gaming technology, a range of web technologies, and the inevitable sticky notes and sketchbooks.

Another key difference in the work of ID and LXD is what you design. Designing an experience is not the same as designing a course, an e-learning module, or a curriculum. They require different methods and tools.

For example, how do you prototype a learning experience? The possibilities are virtually endless. That's why design tools such as experience maps, empathy maps, and personas play a crucial role in LXD when it comes to making the intangible more tangible during the creative process (more in Chapter 7, "Design tools").

A tool is just a tool, of course. Who uses the tool and how they use it determines the quality and nature of the actual outcome. When I introduced the Learning Experience Canvas to a group of primary-school teachers, they simply redistributed everything they normally did to make it fit in the Learning Experience Canvas. They concluded "it's nothing new." When I showed them different ways to use the Learning Experience Canvas, it changed their minds and their designs. Instead of filling existing structures with different content, they were challenged to be creative and generate ideas that focus on the experience of their students. Discovering that learning experiences can come in all shapes and sizes opened their eyes.

Only when you see things differently can
you start doing things differently.

Achieving a mindset shift with educators takes time and effort. The process is similar when I introduce instructional designers to LXD. Understanding learning experience design starts with opening your mind to the possibilities of a design approach.

Results

You can imagine that if you use different perspectives, skills, methods, and tools, you will get different results. And you're right. I see it in the work of the people I train and in different professionals' portfolios. To be clear, one is not better than the other. LXD and ID serve different clients with different needs. For example, many schools and companies want quick and effective solutions that are based on ideas that are tried and tested. For them, ID is probably better.

LXD generally takes more time, as you start from scratch and create a unique design each time. It also requires direct involvement of the client during the design process, which is not always preferred. Clients that are attracted to LXD are willing to try new things because they might feel a standard solution isn't going to get the job done, and they are willing to invest and offer their learners something special. For examples, take a look at case studies in Chapter 8, "Case studies."

LXD and user experience design

User experience design is an essential part of the origins and development of LXD.

There are several similarities between the approach of a learning experience designer and the approach of a user experience designer. At the same time, there are fundamental differences related to what happens when a *user* becomes a *learner*.

LXD and UXD are creative design disciplines. In fact, LXD uses many of the core design principles of UXD. For example, human-centered design and goal-oriented design are common practices in UXD and other creative design disciplines such as interaction design, game design, and graphic design.

When you look at the general design process of creating a user experience, it is like designing a learning experience in many regards. For example, both disciplines use design research, prototyping, and user testing.

In essence, any creative process goes through the same fundamental steps from a first idea to a final design. Like LXD, each design discipline uses versions of the same process to support the type of design you are creating. For example, graphic design doesn't generally conduct user testing, while LXD, UXD, and game design do.

So far, it might sound like UXD and LXD are almost identical. That's not the case. Let's look at some of the fundamental differences between UXD and LXD.

User or learner

A vital lesson I learned when I studied interaction design is this:

A designer is not a typical user.

In other words, you are not the person you design for, so don't assume you know what the user wants or needs. This is a reminder to take design research seriously and to get to know the user before you design for them. In addition, you must become well-versed in what is known about how people learn, and what helps them learn.

A user wants to watch a movie; a learner wants to speak a foreign language

The same applies to UXD and LXD. A learning experience designer is not a typical learner, and a learner is not a user. The needs and goals of a user and a learner are fundamentally different.

A user may want to watch a movie on a streaming service or to use a planning app and not forget birthdays. A learner wants to be able to speak a foreign language, become a more successful entrepreneur, or fulfill requirements to advance a career.

Historically, UXD comes from a task-focused mindset. UXD is about shaping the experience of using a product. LXD is about creating an experience that enables a learner to achieve a desired learning outcome. Both experiences can enrich your life. Having a phone with a great user experience can benefit you greatly. It's not just ease of use. It's about having access to the people and things you love and enjoy.

Having a great learning experience can bring about significant changes in your perspective, knowledge, skills, and behavior. It can benefit you personally, professionally, and academically. They are clearly different outcomes based on different needs and goals.

Researching and mapping out these needs and goals is done in a similar way. For example, creating personas based on design research works well for both UXD and LXD. When you compare user personas and learner personas, you will see that they have a similar structure but different content. For a learner, I would include levels of cognitive, social, physical, and emotional development. That wouldn't always be necessary for a user, certainly not in such detail and only as it relates to using a specific product or service.

Users are faced with different choices than learners

Both fields use cognitive psychology to understand what motivates people and to explain the choices they make. Users are faced with different choices than learners. Also, the rationale motivating their choices is different. For example, during a one-year training program, a learner goes through a complex psychological process where the level of motivation can vary greatly. Understanding what the learner goes through and offering a learning experience that motivates, engages, and empowers them are key aspects of successful LXD.

A different experience

User experience design focuses on the interaction a user has with a product or service. For example, think about all the steps you take when you book a flight. A large part of that process goes through apps and websites, from searching for plane tickets to paying. In general, UXD is essential for digital (online) experiences.

LXD has a broad scope because of the many ways people learn. A learning experience can be a high-tech interactive digital experience or one that uses no technology at all. I've worked on a wide variety of designs using elements such as (board) games, music, apps, e-learning, physical exercise, theater, virtual, and public spaces. The possibilities are endless.

Learning experiences and user experiences can be very different in terms of scale and scope. In general, learning experiences can have a higher level of complexity and variety when it comes to the design choices you make. The challenge of UXD is often to engage a user that might, at any moment, abandon the experience. Both UXD and LXD require talented designers to deliver a high-quality experience.

Easy or challenging

The main goal of a UX designer is to create an experience that is as simple and easy as possible. You try to take away any friction or confusion for a smooth and elegant user experience.

A great user experience is effortless;
a great learning experience is challenging.

The essence of learning is to challenge yourself and exceed your previous abilities and grow. These challenges are hard by default. If it's easy, you're not really learning. Personal growth is a continuous and challenging process, and as a learning experience designer, you try to provide the right level of challenge. Too much challenge and the learner will feel frustrated. Not enough challenge and the learner gets bored. In this regard, game design is a great source of inspiration for LXD. Good games are great at providing just the right level of challenge.

LXD and design thinking

Design thinking often comes up when people talk about LXD. The rise in popularity of design thinking in business and education has contributed to the success of LXD.

While there are links between design thinking and LXD, they cannot easily be compared.

The field of design used to be like an island — a magical place where creative people gathered to make things look, feel, and work better. It is a great place to be if you're a designer but not very accessible for people without a design background.

Nowadays design is everywhere. Designers have left the island to apply their talents in all kinds of places. Before, design was exclusively used to create things such as posters, book covers, interfaces, fashion, and furniture. Today, designers create services, events, environments, and learning experiences.

This cross-over from design into other fields has fostered the rise of design thinking. It has built a bridge from the island of design and allows designers and non-designers to understand each other better and collaborate. That's good news, but it has made it harder to distinguish the application of design thinking from design disciplines like LXD.

Design thinking is a methodology for creative problem solving. Traditionally, problem solving uses a methodical, almost scientific approach. This methodical scientific approach is one of the core qualities of disciplines in the field of learning like instructional design. These disciplines use applied scientific principles for effective instruction, to support learning, and to improve performance.

Design thinking uses a fundamentally different approach, which is less methodical and more about exploring, experimenting, empathizing, and creating. LXD is a design discipline just like user experience design, interaction design, and graphic design. These are the fields that have inspired design thinking. When you see similarities between LXD and design thinking, it's because design thinking uses elements that come from design disciplines. And LXD is a design discipline!

You don't have to be a learning experience designer to benefit from elements of LXD. If you come from the field of learning, you can enhance your classes, courses, or training by using design thinking. For example, as a teacher, you can use design thinking to apply human-centered design principles when you redesign one of your classes. This will offer valuable benefits and will surely improve the experiences of your learners. This is well worth doing but is not the same as working as a qualified learning experience designer.

The learning experience designer

Who you are as a designer, how you proceed, and which tools you use determine the kind of learning experiences you are able to design.

There are three vital parts of learning experience design: the designer, the design process, and the design tools (**FIGURE 3.6**).

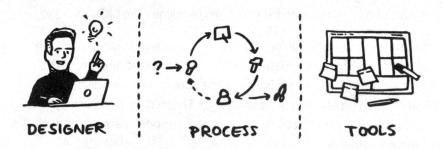

FIGURE 3.6 *We'll see this graphic again when we focus on process and tools.*

In this chapter, we are going to consider the role of the designer. This section is about what it takes to be a learning experience designer and how LXD relates to you. In the later chapters, we'll explore the design process and the design tools you need to apply LXD successfully.

At a basic level anybody can design a learning experience. We do it all the time, even if we are not aware of it. Just think about the learning experience you offer to your spouse, kids, friends, or family, not as a professional but as a partner, parent, friend, or relative.

You take your kids to a museum and share your love for early 20th-century European art. You recommend a book that lifted your spirits to a friend who's feeling down. You have a meaningful conversation with your aunt and give her some valuable advice. You help your partner prepare for an important presentation and give feedback that boosts their confidence.

These are all examples of the learning experiences we have in our daily lives. They are positive, personal, and profound experiences that benefit other people.

By now you might wonder, if anyone can design a learning experience, why read this book? What's the use of being a learning experience designer?

We're not talking about designing just any learning experience. We are talking about designing specific learning experiences that tackle complex challenges by creating unique designs. At my design firm, we are used to working with a wide variety of clients that expect us to deal with anything they throw at us. Also, the designs we create are always different from any previous designs because no two learners are the same and no two projects are the same. This requires professional design skills, a tried and tested creative process, and the tools that enable you to do your best work.

I sometimes feel people underestimate what it takes to be a learning experience designer. Nobody expects to become a graphic designer or game designer overnight, yet I see people change their job title to LX designer without really changing their approach. Maybe LXD just sounds exciting, or they might feel it better reflects what they would like to do. Either way, I believe it's important to have a decent understanding and mastery of LXD before you call yourself a learning experience designer.

When you start to apply the principles, methods, and tools of LXD in a design process, you will come across many challenges. This book supports you in tackling these challenges on your way to mastering LXD.

Qualities of a learning experience designer

A learning experience designer is a creative professional who uses design skills, methods, and tools to design experiences that enable people to learn.

What exactly do you have to be able to do to be successful at that?

To answer this question, I took a good look at the things that myself and my team have been doing to satisfy the needs of the learners we design for. I've also looked at the many people I've trained and analyzed what they have mastered on their path to becoming learning experience designers. As a result, I came up with eight things a learning experience designer should be able to do:

1. Use creativity as a driving force.

LXD is a design discipline. As a designer, you use your creative talent to come up with original ideas, conceptualize these ideas, and find the right shape or form for your design. Creativity is not only the spark that ignites a design session but also the fuel for the complete design process.

2. Have a creative and analytical mindset.

The design process of a learning experience requires different mindsets. You are switching between analytical and creative as you do your research and then create, test, and improve your design. The ability to adapt your mindset allows you to be effective throughout the design process and get the best of both worlds.

3. Let go of what you know.

We all have preconceived notions of what learning is like. These notions are based on our own experiences in school and at work. It's easy to fall into the trap of designing similar experiences and not benefit from the endless opportunities to shape the way we learn. Try to let go of what you know and use your creative freedom to do things differently.

4. Focus on the learner.

Human-centered design is a big part of creating effective and engaging learning experiences. Being able to empathize with the learner enables you to design a more personal learning experience that really works. Never forget that the learner is always the most important person in your work.

5. Incorporate (neuro)scientific insights.

Understanding how our brain works and how we learn enables you to create designs that are effective in helping the learner reach their goals. You have to be able to learn from and work with (neuro)scientists to incorporate their precious insights and knowledge into your designs.

6. Be both practical and imaginative.

Learning experience designers push boundaries and try to find innovative and elegant solutions for complex problems. At the same time, you want to keep things as simple and as practical as possible for your design to work in a real-life situation. Try to balance your craziest ideas with a healthy dose of realism.

7. Choose the right technology.

Learning is not about technology; it's about people and their goals. The technology you choose is based on what will enable the learner to reach their desired learning outcome. Choosing the technology that serves this purpose is a vital part of designing a great learning experience. Using technology is always a means to an end and not a goal in itself.

8. Align different perspectives.

An LXD project can involve a variety of stakeholders, such as learners, clients, experts, scientists, or software developers. They all have different needs and desires. It is your responsibility to unite these people by aligning their perspectives and creating a learning experience that works for all of them.

Your path to mastering LXD

LXD is an interdisciplinary field that attracts people from all kinds of backgrounds. Just like you, we all have our unique path into the field of LXD and toward mastering LXD.

Who you are and where you come from determines what you are good at and what might need to be improved if you want to be successful at designing learning experiences.

There are a wide variety of educational, creative, and other professionals who are attracted to the ideas, methods, and tools of LXD. I've met and trained quite a few of them.

They include teachers looking for ways to motivate their students, trainers who want to offer a more engaging training program, publishers who want to go beyond traditional solutions, instructional designers looking for a fresh perspective and new skills, and experience designers who want to gain insights into the specific needs of learners to apply their skills to educational projects.

This colorful group of people have two things in common: passion for learning and a need to find better ways of learning.

When you look at the four quadrants that are used to define LXD, it's important to know where you would position yourself (**FIGURE 3.7**). If you know which areas you've mastered, it's easy to see the parts that are missing. Ideally, you're able to cover all four quadrants, but first you need to know your starting point.

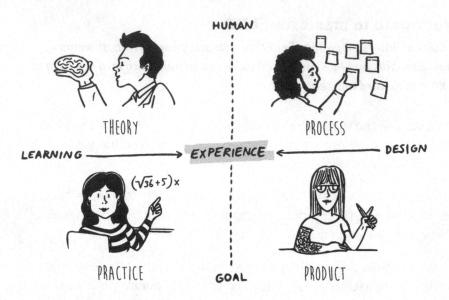

FIGURE 3.7 *Learning experience designer: quadrants summarized.*

Let's take a look at all of the four quadrants in more detail and see who you identify with the most.

PROCESS: Human side of design

You are used to offering people an experience that gets them where they want to go in an enjoyable way.

With a user-centered approach, you have your eye on the people you design for. You take their goals, wants, needs, and doubts and merge them into a complete, logical, and pleasant experience. Since you are used to incorporating elements of (cognitive) psychology in your designs, you are familiar with the more scientific side of design. Add user research and user testing and it's clear that you combine both analytical and creative skills.

The practical aspects of designing an experience for an environment where people learn, such as a school or training space, can be challenging. There are many written and unwritten rules within education that you need to take into account. For example, primary-school teachers are generally short on time. They have full classes of students and a lot to do. When you create a design that they will implement in the classroom, it needs to be quick and easy for them or you'll lose them straightaway.

Feeling at home in these environments by knowing and understanding the people who learn and work here, such as students, teachers, trainers, managers, principals, and publishers, is essential.

PRODUCT: Goal-oriented design

You can take an idea and turn it into a shape or form that people can relate to. Your designs can communicate a message, provide functionality, work easily, and are aesthetically pleasing.

People like what they see and enjoy interacting with your designs, whether it's a physical object, a visual design, or a game. Your ability to generate original ideas helps you to create innovative and authentic designs. When standard educational products fall short in achieving the specific goals you want to achieve, it's your time to shine.

Designing a product that is used in a learning experience requires a specific set of skills. It's just one part of the experience and choosing the right medium or technology for your design can be challenging. Being able to do this is a core quality of a learning experience designer.

The goals your design enables learners to achieve can be diverse. The priorities of the learner are your main concern, but each stakeholder also has their own goals. Aligning and achieving those goals through the design you create are the best measure of success.

THEORY: Human side of learning

Studying the human brain and behavior is key to understanding how people learn.

Use a scientific approach to explain what motivates people to do the things they do. Through this understanding you are able to provide a theoretical foundation for people who put learning into practice. This foundation helps you to make thought-out choices on how to support learners in reaching their goals. Measuring and validating experiences can clarify if and why a learning experience might work.

The world of science can sometimes be disconnected from the real world. It's a shame when theory can't be put into practice. Finding a practical application for theoretical insights is of great value to the learner.

LXD requires both analytical and creative skills to design a learning experience. Being able to tap into your creative side is going to make a big difference when it comes to creating better learning experiences. If a scientific mindset is your strength, developing creative skills can be challenging, but don't let that hold you down. Just look at Leonardo da Vinci who combined arts and science in an incredible way.

PRACTICE: Goal-oriented learning

You are a learning professional who is dedicated to the learner. Your students or trainees get the attention and guidance they need for their personal growth and development.

You have the experience, tools, and tricks to provide education in a way that helps them reach their goals and push their boundaries. The educational system is well known to you with all of its possibilities and limitations.

Letting go of the ideas and methods that you are used to in education is going to be hard. It's not that you are doing everything wrong, definitely not. It's just that you could be doing things differently if needed. Sometimes you'll have to leave your comfort zone, forget what you know, and start from scratch.

This can be both liberating and frightening at the same time. Just give it a try and you'll be amazed at all there is to learn and enjoy.

Who are you?

When you look at the four types of professionals we just discussed, who do you identify with the most? And what does that mean?

Chances are that you identify most as one type of professional. That is your starting point for your journey into the field of LXD. Now you know which of these quadrants is covered by your current expertise. For example, if you're a user experience designer, process design is one of your strengths. Or you might be an instructional designer; in that case your ability to put learning into practice is a strength.

Each quadrant has its own strengths and weaknesses. As a user experience designer you might be challenged by implementing learning theory in your design. As an instructional designer you might struggle with the creative design side of LXD.

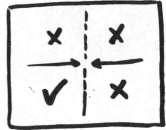

Maybe, your expertise covers more than one quadrant right now. You could be a graphic designer who teaches or a neuroscientist who designs games. In that case, you have a head start. There is less ground to cover, and you have experienced the challenges and benefits of crossing over into new territory firsthand.

Being aware of what you're good at, what is lacking and what your challenges are is essential for mastering LXD. Be proud of what you've already achieved and be honest about what you have yet to learn or unlearn.

The only source of knowledge is experience. You need experience to gain wisdom.

— ALBERT EINSTEIN, PHYSICIST

Chapter 4

Experiential learning

ESSENTIALS

How do we learn from experience? This is a key question for learning experience designers. The answer can be found in the field of experiential learning.

When I studied graphic design, I had an art teacher who was feared by his students. He was an angry man who was very strict. If you were one minute late, which could easily happen to me since I traveled by train, you were not allowed to enter the studio. Nobody liked him, and half the time we didn't really know what we were doing. In the first lesson we had to draw dots and lines for hours (**FIGURE 4.1**). If you joked about it, he exploded and yelled, "This may not look serious to you, but it is for me!" His methods made little sense to me at first, but eventually they would.

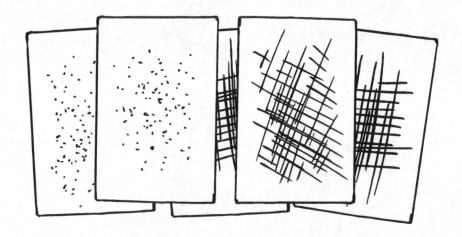

FIGURE 4.1 *Drawing dots and lines for hours seemed senseless at first.*

Long after his lessons, near the end of my study, I ran into him in the hall-way. I asked if he had a moment because I wanted to thank him. I told him that as weird as his lessons were, they made me think about how drawing is more than putting a piece of charcoal on a sheet of paper. It is about what you see and how to translate that into an image. Seeing things from different angles, and the ability to capture what you envision into some-thing tangible, is elemental to being a designer. As I thanked him for these valuable lessons, he got emotional. With teary eyes he replied, "I'm just passionate about what I teach, and I'm so glad you get it; that means a lot to me, thank you."

This experience changed me. It went far beyond acquiring the skill of drawing or knowing about composition and arts and crafts materials. I gained valuable insights that changed my views. I became a different designer, a different person.

Experiences have the power to change how we see things, what we know, what we do, and who we are. The four elements of seeing, knowing, doing, and being are foundational to experiential learning.

Experiential learning theory

The field of experiential learning studies how we learn from experience. Unlike popular belief, it is not just about learning by doing.

Experiential learning is frequently explained as "learning by doing." If you want to learn what to do, you must do what you learn. While this makes sense, it doesn't do justice to the science and tradition of experiential learning.

The field of experiential learning has been shaped by several inspiring people such as John Dewey, Jean Piaget, Kurt Lewin, and David A. Kolb. At the heart of their work, you will find theories about how we experience and how we learn from our experience. They came up with models that explain how all experiences go through cycles in a few universal steps.

When you look at these models of experiential learning, they look similar. The main variations are in the terminology they use. These similarities aren't surprising since they were inspired by each other's work. I humbly walked in their footsteps and created my own model based on their incredible work. That's for later, though. First, let's explore the four elements that are the foundation of experiential learning.

Four elements of experiential learning

When you look at the different models that were developed over the years in the field of experiential learning, there are four universal elements: concrete, abstract, active, and reflective (**FIGURE 4.2**).

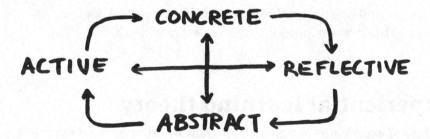

FIGURE 4.2 *The four experiential elements.*

Two things are important to notice here:

- First, it is a cyclical model. Every experience goes through a cycle of four steps.

- Second, there are two pairs of opposites in this model. *Concrete* is the opposite of *abstract*, and *reflective* is the opposite of *active*.

Let me give you an example of a common experience and explain what happens in each of the four steps.

1. A girl goes to the toy store. This is the first step, a **concrete** situation.

2. She sees a LEGO set she likes and wonders if she wants to buy it. This is a **reflective** observation. The price is $25, and she looks in her wallet to count her money. Numbers and money are **abstract** concepts, and her knowledge of adding numbers is needed to decide what to do. She figures out that she has $32.

3. She happily purchases the LEGO set. Making a choice and taking action are the **active** parts of the cycle.

4. She goes home happy and can't wait to play with her new toy. This is the start of a new **concrete** experience.

Buying the LEGO set changed her, not just emotionally, although she is indeed happy and excited. She also learned a lesson on why it's important to save up money instead of spending it straightaway. The experiential cycle continues, and each cycle changes you in one way or the other.

Before we dig deeper into this cycle and each of its elements, let's talk about learning styles. You can imagine that some people may prefer to learn in a practical way that is concrete and active, where others enjoy a theoretical approach that is more abstract and reflective.

This is the basis for the concept of learning styles — which is a bit of a controversial topic. While it makes sense to look at individual talents and the preferences of learners, I don't believe that it makes sense to categorize learners based on specific learning styles:

- People don't have just one learning style; that's a simplification of the learner and the process of learning.

- Instead of treating the four elements separately, you should treat them as a whole.

Human experience consists of concrete, abstract, reflective, and active elements — it's the nature of experience. Separating these elements is unnatural and irrational. Let's look at how these opposite elements relate to each other.

Concrete to abstract

Our daily life consists of a series of concrete experiences, such as having breakfast, going to work, playing with the kids, and so on. These experiences are quite ordinary, but not when we think about them on a more abstract level:

- What is the nutritional value of my breakfast?

- What are the benefits and downsides of different modes of transportation?

- Why is the game I'm playing with my kids such a great game?

Answering these kinds of questions requires some level of abstraction. Science gives us theoretical explanations for things that happen in the real world. For example, physics has ways to explain how gravity works. While every human being knows that objects fall down instead of up, not everyone can explain exactly why and how this works.

Being able to look at events at different levels of abstraction will enable you to gain a deeper and clearer understanding of the world we live in. However, when abstract concepts are not relatable to real-world situations, they lose their relevance. There can be a disconnect between the scientific community and the rest of the world when their work is perceived to have no practical application.

This disconnect can also exist within learning experiences. If a learner is provided only with theories, models, and facts that have no real application, it's hard for them to see how they relate to their situation. That's why it's easier to teach kids how to add and subtract by using real-world objects like apples. Seeing how one apple plus another apple makes two apples makes sense to the child.

On the other hand, if adults needed apples to perform addition or subtraction, we'd be in deep trouble. There is a need for higher levels of abstraction if you want to participate in modern society and perform certain jobs.

Balancing concrete and abstract aspects of your learning experiences is the crux of the challenge. Simply put, make sure theory can be applied and practical matters can be explained.

Reflective to active

When you are faced with doing something you've never done before, what would you do:

- Just try it and see what happens?

- Watch and wait before you try anything?

If you just try it, you might succeed. This could be so-called beginner's luck, or maybe you're just talented. Either way, it shows you have an active mindset. If you watch and wait, chances are that you might find the right strategy to be successful before you take any action. This shows you have a more reflective mindset.

One is not better than the other. Simply trying things without over-thinking them can work wonders. Sometimes you may not have the luxury to contemplate for long when you are an entrepreneur and you see a golden opportunity to seize. Other times taking some time to observe a situation and trying to figure out what to do next can help you make balanced choices. That's why that same entrepreneur studies the competition and writes a business plan.

It's obvious that both reflective and active behavior can be great assets in life in general and in learning. Learning, by definition, requires you to do something you haven't done before. This requires learners to observe, think, act, and reflect.

For learning experiences it's crucial to include both active and reflective elements. In traditional education these elements are often separated. This makes it harder to learn, especially as they are opposites: reflection is an internal process, while action is an external process.

Action and reflection both can provide you with valuable feedback. This enables you to adjust your actions when necessary. Game design is renowned for using feedback effectively. When you play a game, you get instant and continuous feedback on your actions. Whether it's from rolling a die or pressing a button on your controller, you know straightaway what consequences come from your action.

For me game design is a great source of inspiration. I frequently use game elements to enhance a learning experience, and I advise you to explore this field as well. It's great fun and extremely useful. Game on!

Be, see, know, and do

Can we look at the process of experiential learning and focus on what the learner is doing?

We've discussed different models that consider and conceptualize how we experience. Keeping the human, the learner, at the center, I looked at bringing these models together in a clear, simple way.

The result is a four-step process that illustrates how we experience on a universal and fundamental level: by being, seeing, knowing, and doing (**FIGURE 4.3**).

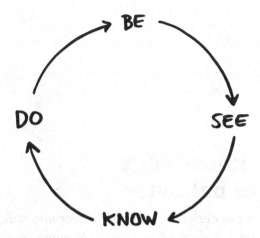

FIGURE 4.3 *My simpler four-step cyclical process focused on what actions the learner engages in.*

Be

Be is about who you are and what you feel. It emphasizes feeling as opposed to thinking. It is about being involved in real and concrete situations as a human being.

See

See is about how you view yourself and the world around you.

It emphasizes understanding as opposed to practical application. It is about understanding the meaning of ideas and situations through observation and reflection.

Know

Know is about the knowledge you possess and gain. It emphasizes thinking as opposed to feeling. It focuses on how you take in facts and data and then process it on a conceptual and theoretical level.

Do

Do is about the actions you take and the choices you make.

It emphasizes practical application as opposed to understanding. It is about actively influencing people and changing situations.

Insight, knowledge, skill, and behavior

An important part of designing experiential learning is defining learning objectives. There are four types of learning objectives: insight, knowledge, skill, and behavior.

The four types of learning objectives can be connected to the four quadrants in our "be, see, know, and do" model (**FIGURE 4.4**).

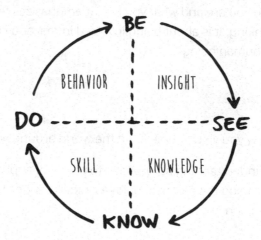

FIGURE 4.4 *The four types of learning objectives are based on my cyclical experiential model.*

Traditionally there's a focus in education on knowledge and skill that can be evaluated. In my opinion, this doesn't do justice to how we learn from what we experience. If you gain new knowledge without having the proper perspective, it will be hard to process and appreciate. If you acquire knowledge without the ability to apply it, it will be less relevant and easily forgotten.

Learning from experience happens in a four-part cycle of being, seeing, knowing, and doing, every single time. By simply leaving out one or more parts, you break this cycle. This means you dismiss the dynamics of how people learn from what they experience and offer them a limited representation of reality.

The dynamics of how we experience the world around us using insight, knowledge, skill, and behavior provide vital insights for LXD.

Understanding this allows for designing more holistic, natural, and personal experiences. To illustrate these dynamics, let's consider the example of a walk in the forest.

Walking in a forest

Consider this scenario:

- You are walking in a forest.

- After some time, you take a good look around (SEE).

- As you reflect on what you see, you come to the conclusion that you are lost (insight).

- There's no need to panic because your father once taught you how to navigate using the sun as a compass, and you know that the sun rises in the east and sets in the west (knowledge, KNOW).

- You look at the time of day and the position of the sun, and you are able to determine north, east, south, and west (skill).

- You start walking in the right direction (DO).

- After a long detour you find your way back and you're tired but relieved (BE).

- You promise yourself to be a bit more careful next time and not get lost in the first place (behavior).

What you see in this example is how any experience begins and ends with certain behavior. Actual change requires new insights, knowledge, skills, and behavior for the learner. When you design any type of learning experience, you'll want to include all four types of learning objectives.

Always think about the learner

Often, clients want a learning experience to cover certain knowledge or teach a new skill. Or they might want to change specific behavior. I always explain that you can't have one without the other. If people acquire new knowledge but don't apply it on the job, it's useless. If you learned a new skill but you don't see how it is relevant, you won't use this skill. If your views have changed but you don't know how to turn this into a behavioral change, you're lost.

Always think about who the learner is, how they see things, what they know, and what they do.

And when you define learning objectives, ensure that the learner demonstrates the right insights, knowledge, skill, and behavior in the end.

This chapter is just a brief introduction to the deep subject of how we learn. It gives you an idea of all that learning experience designers must consider that is specific to the process of learning.

*A mind is like a parachute;
it doesn't work unless it's open.*

— FRANK ZAPPA, MUSICIAN

Chapter 5

How to
design a
learning
experience THAT'S
MEMORABLE
UNIQUE
ENGAGING
PERSONAL
EFFECTIVE
AUTHENTIC
SURPRISING

You probably can't wait to put learning experience design (LXD) into action. That's great! Designing learning experiences is an exciting, challenging, fun, and fulfilling process.

Remember, we established three vital elements of designing a learning experience: the designer, the design process, and the design tools (**FIGURE 5.1**).

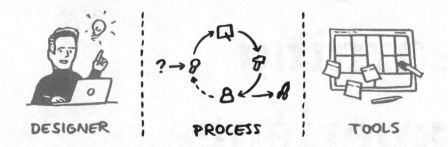

FIGURE 5.1 *Understanding the design process enables you to get the most out of your designer's skill and tools.*

We've talked about the designer, and before we focus on design tools, we'll dive deep into the design process. Understanding the design process enables you to get the most out of your design skills and tools. Going through a design process is fun but never easy. You will come across many challenges. This book supports you in tackling these challenges.

Let go of what you know

If you paint a picture in your mind of someone learning, what does that actually look like? Does it involve a teacher in a classroom? Is it a student hitting the books? Or someone watching YouTube videos?

We all have preconceived notions of what learning looks like. The first thought that comes to mind is often quite traditional and predictable, like a teacher educating students. It's what we are used to from our own experience. Obviously, there are many ways to learn. In fact, the possibilities are so numerous that the best thing to do right now is to let go of what you know.

Letting go of your assumptions about what learning looks like is necessary to find the space you need to be creative. Assumptions will only limit your creativity, and as a designer, that's counterproductive.

Just to be clear, there is value in what you know!

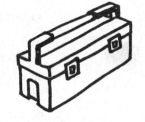

Take an imaginary toolbox and put your knowledge in there so you can take it out later when it comes in handy. Just like in a real toolbox, your knowledge consists of tools to craft a learning experience. It's a matter of finding the right tools for the job.

If you know best how to use a hammer, every solution to your problems is a nail. This analogy hits the nail right on the head, so to speak, when it comes to one of the biggest challenges you may face right now: going with what you know. It's time to open your mind and think freely.

I've seen this happen many times when I conduct workshops. There is a common tendency to "invent" with solutions that you already know. You may remember a certain activity that could work just as well for this situation — you are done before you get started. That's a burden that comes with prior experience. Our frame of reference can become rigid and disable us from seeing new opportunities from a fresh perspective.

Being a learning experience designer is all about creating original designs and inventing a unique something that works perfectly for a specific situation. Recycling ideas is never original, and while it can work, you're better off coming up with ideas of your own.

Being serious about creating original work based on your ideas will unlock your creative potential. It will put you on a path to a more enjoyable and rewarding design process.

The learning experience design process

There are various ways to design a learning experience. It can be an unpredictable and adventurous process. This unpredictability is in a way inherent to the creative, agile, and innovative approach learning experience designers use.

When you focus on the fundamentals of the design process, there are six basic steps you need to take, which we will explore in this chapter. At its core, it is an iterative process with the same steps that other design disciplines use. But when you dig deeper, you will uncover aspects of the design process that are unique to the process of creating a learning experience.

We'll begin with a quick overview of the process, as shown in **FIGURE 5.2**.

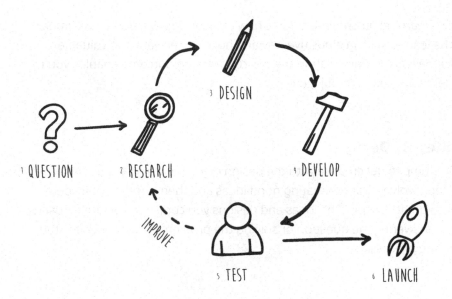

FIGURE 5.2 *Note how the process may cycle a few times before launch.*

Step 1: Question

You start with a question you want to answer or a problem you want to solve. Formulating the right question is essential for a good design process. It is your dot on the horizon, the goal you are reaching for. Having the right question to start will ensure you are heading in the right direction.

Step 2: Research

There are at least two things you need to research before you can design a learning experience: the learner and the learning outcome.

Conducting research into the people who will learn from the experience that you're designing is a key part of the design process.

The learning outcome describes how the learning experience will impact the learners' life in a positive way and how it is relevant and valuable to the learner. Formulating the desired learning outcome enables you to define the learning objectives.

Step 3: Design

It is time to get creative with the design of your learning experience. This step involves first generating good ideas and then turning those ideas into great designs. The ideas and designs you come up with are focused on answering the question or solving the problems you defined in step 1 of the process.

Step 4: Develop

In the development phase, you take your design and turn it into an actual experience. You start by developing a first prototype. The kind of prototype you develop depends on the type of experience that you're designing. With each design iteration, you develop a more detailed and finalized version of your learning experience.

Step 5: Test

Does your design work? Let's put it to the test to figure out what learning objectives are reached by the learner and if the actual learning outcome is achieved. Also, does your design appeal to the learner? Keep in mind that testing a prototype works differently than testing a fully developed learning experience.

Step 6: Launch

Once you've developed the final learning experience, you're ready to launch. A lot has happened before you get to this point. Going from the first ideas, rough sketches, and rapid prototype to a fully tested final design takes several iterations.

Every time you go through the cycle of the design process, you come closer to launching. You might wonder, when am I ready to launch? Basically, you need to repeat this cycle until you, the learner, and the other stakeholders are satisfied with the results.

Now, let's look at each of these steps in more detail.

Question

When you start the process of designing a learning experience, it's important to clarify what you are trying to achieve. The need for a clear goal is obvious, but formulating that goal is not always easy.

As a learning experience designer, you work for a wide variety of clients. Each client has their own question for you. Here are some examples: Our company needs agile training. Our university needs to change our international affairs course to an online course. Our organization wants an e-learning module on digital marketing.

It's your job not only to answer these questions but also to figure out if these are the right questions to begin with. Often the wish of the client is not what the learners need. In fact, it is often not what the client needs. By digging deeper into the needs of the learner, the client, and other stakeholders, you can start to define the deeper, more fundamental questions you want to answer.

Asking the right questions

How do you know whether the question you are trying to answer is the right question to ask? A simple and effective way to start is by asking why the client would like to know the answer to this question.

Let me give you an example of a question from a physics teacher.

Teacher: Many of my students struggle in my physics classes. Can you design a physics game for them?

LX designer: Why would you want to use a game instead of anything else?

Teacher: Because kids like games and it motivates them.

LX designer: Is motivation the main reason they struggle?

Teacher: I guess, they think it is boring.

LX designer: Is it boring?

Teacher: Of course not! It's a fascinating field with so many interesting and fun things to learn.

LX designer: Sounds great; why don't the students share this perspective?

Teacher: I'm not sure. Maybe physics is a bit abstract or complex for them. They don't really see how it relates to them.

LX designer: So, they don't perceive it as relevant?

Teacher: No. They don't know why they must learn physics.

LX designer: What we are trying to achieve here is to make physics more relevant and therefore more meaningful to the students. This can increase engagement, motivation, and performance.

Teacher: I agree, but how do we do that?

LX designer: That's a good question. A game could work, but that's hard to predict. My job is to figure out what type of experience would be relevant, meaningful, and motivating. Let's start by discussing what you love about physics, and we'll take it from there.

As you can see, there are many different questions you can ask about the same topic. Often there are assumptions in our questions that limit the possibilities of designing a great learning experience. By having a clear question to begin with, you are off to a great start.

Sometimes the answer to the question isn't learning.

Five whys

There is a method that is as simple as it is effective for getting to the core of a question: the five whys.

This is how it works: When you get the answer to a question, simply ask, "Why?" This leads to a new answer, which in turn leads to you asking "Why?" again. After asking "Why?" five times, you probably have a more profound answer to your question. Here's an example:

I'm looking forward to reading this book because I want to learn more about LXD. Why?

LXD skills are important to me as a professional. Why?

Because it will keep my skills up to date and enable me to design better learning experiences. Why?

I want my students to benefit from the experiences I design. Why?

Because my students matter to me and I want to provide them with the best possible learning experiences. Why?

I want my students to succeed in school and in life, and I believe LXD will enable me to contribute to both their and my success.

Awesome!

Research

A well-designed learning experience is based on thorough research. By doing research, you gain a deeper understanding and empathy for the learner and their goals.

Let's look at why research is an indispensable part of the learning experience design process. As an interaction design student, I learned that a designer is not a typical user. This design mantra is a constant reminder that you are not the same as the people you design for. This is because not only are you almost by definition in a different demographic than your users, but also because a designer looks at a design differently than a nondesigner.

You are not the person you design for

In the case of interaction design, you spend a lot of time worrying about things such as navigational structures, information architecture, feedback, and visual aspects like color schemes, font sizes, and layout. A user doesn't care about any of this. They are interested only in reaching their goals and getting to a desirable outcome. The catch here is that it's just so easy and seductive to think you know better, and you're doing the user a service by deciding what's best for them.

This is also the case for learning experience designers. You are not the person you design for. As a learning experience designer, your purpose is to serve the learner, and the only way to do that right is by having a clear picture of who the learner is and what their goals are.

Research enables you to do the following:

- Understand the people you design for.

- Have empathy for the people you design for.

- Think about the learner instead of thinking for the learner.

- Formulate a learning outcome that is relevant and meaningful to the learner.

- Formulate learning objectives that enable the learner to reach their desired learning outcome.

- Work with credible data instead of assumptions and guesses.

- Have more certainty in the design choices you make.

- Create a design that is truly personal and authentic.

There are many ways to do research. You don't always need years of scientific research before you can start to work on your design. What you do need is an effective approach. I've selected a number of research methods that I've used many times. Most of the time I use a combination of these methods for my design research. Take a good look at them and see what would work best for you and your learners.

Desktop research

A lot of research has already been done and is available for you to learn from. Gather all the data that's insightful for you such as reports, statistics, and demographics from your desktop using reading material online or in books. This type of data is ideal for quantitative research and very time effective.

I typically use desktop research to obtain an overview and a frame of reference. This can be both topic-related and learner-related. For example, when you design a learning experience about computer skills for elderly people in Greece, you want to know what and who you are dealing with. Using desktop research to gather demographics and general knowledge about computer skills is a good starting point. To complete the research, you want to do contextual observation or interviews, which will be discussed in a moment.

Where do you start looking? You can go either online or offline. Either way, the data you gather must be valid, which means that you must use trusted sources such as libraries, universities, research centers, governments, or experts. Using social media for gathering data probably isn't a good idea unless you're doing online ethnography (there's more about this in the next section).

Online resources are virtually endless. Having a search strategy can help focus your attention. Think about the keywords you want to include and exclude in a search. Use websites that can filter and represent data in a usable way.

Traditional resources like books can also be great for research. With online resources being easily accessible, we sometimes forget the value and practicality of books. Unlike a single report or article, books generally incorporate many different findings from different sources in one convenient place.

Once you've gathered data, you want to be able to share and present your findings. A great way to do that is by creating a chart or an infographic. A quicker way is to create a word cloud. There are free online tools available for that. You can also take it one step further by creating an interactive infographic or animation. The shape or form you choose depends on budget allocation, time available, and type of research you've done.

Online ethnography

Immerse yourself in an online community and experience firsthand what's happening in the world of your learners. Traditionally, ethnography was done in real-world communities — this is easier and cheaper.

Online communities can offer a wealth of knowledge about a certain group of people and a specific topic. The upside to this approach is that you can easily get access to the people you design for. The downside is that you have to invest quite some time to get to know them and figure out who they are and what their needs are.

In 2016, when myself and my team organized the first LXD conference, we created a LinkedIn group about LXD. Over time that group has grown to thousands of members. I have studied the activity in this group to learn more about what attracts people to LXD, what their most common questions are, and what kind of support they need to be successful at LXD. It's not just about keeping track of what's being posted; I also interacted with the community to dig deeper. Having conversations with members, responding to questions, and creating polls were all highly insightful.

Writing this book is partly based on the lessons I learned from being a member of that group. People would frequently ask, "Is there a book on LXD?" At the same time, there appears to be a need for clarity on the topic of LXD and some practical advice on how to design a learning experience. When you combine this need with insights about where the members come from and what profession they have, you can start to paint a more detailed picture of who these people are and how best to serve them.

For this type of research, you can watch from the sidelines and simply observe what's happening. You can also interact with the people you are researching. In that case, you want to be open and honest about your motives. You want to earn trust, and honesty is essential for that.

Questionnaires

A tried and tested way to gather loads of quantitative data and some qualitative data is a questionnaire.

When I create a questionnaire, the first step is to prioritize the questions you want to ask. Generally, you want to know how the topic or goal of your design is perceived and valued by the learner. The trick is to ask very specific questions and keep it as short as possible, but not too short.

You also want to think about when and where to conduct questionnaires. I love to create a quick first questionnaire at the beginning of a project to get a general idea of who and what you're dealing with. This is useful in refining the question you're trying to answer and formulating the learning outcome.

I like to go straight to where the learners are to conduct questionnaires. Let's say you are designing a learning experience about customer service for store employees. Just go to local stores and ask them to fill out the questionnaires. Even if you are working for a client with types of stores that are not near to you, going to any store will be better than not going at all.

If you don't have your target audience nearby, you can also use online questionnaires and send them to people in your network or post them in online communities, forums, or social networks.

Contextual observation

See how learners act in their natural environment by using contextual observation. This is my favorite research method because it is as real and authentic as it gets.

Whenever I get the chance, I love to go into the field and see the learner in action. Doing this allows you to broaden your perspective on the learner and their goals. At the same time, it enables you to dig deeper into the psyche and behavior of the learner as they behave naturally.

One time I visited a school together with an educational publisher and a software developer. We all saw the same students do the same things. Yet when we discussed our findings, it turned out that I had noticed many things that they didn't register at all. Their focus was practical and already on how a possible solution was going to work in this environment. My focus was on trying to find the right problem. That's why I carefully looked at how the students were behaving, what they enjoyed, what they disliked, and how they felt at different moments in time. As a result, I was able to connect with both the learners and the teachers on a cognitive and emotional level.

Part of being a designer is being sensitive to the people and world around you and being able to pick up on things that others don't. Use that sensibility to understand the people you design for, empathize with them, and find ways to best serve and support them.

Interviews

Take the time to sit down and carefully listen to someone's story. Conducting an interview is a wonderful way to get to know the learner, talk to experts, and dig deeper into the areas that are most relevant to them and to you as a designer.

If you've ever been interviewed, you know that the questions are just as important as the answers. It starts with sincere interest in another person. Be curious! Ask open questions (why, where, how, etc.). Don't interpret but ask further; for instance: "You say that this book is really interesting. What do you find interesting about it?" How you interpret words is another pitfall, but asking what the learner means with a certain word can also be a breakthrough. A good interview leads to a great conversation and to gathering valuable information.

A potential pitfall is to simply go down a list of questions that you've prepared. Rather, focus on a limited number of topics that you want to discuss. Use a handful of well-prepared questions to address a new topic, but don't let the questions alone guide you. This can prevent you from asking follow-up questions and make you miss out on vital information.

The topics you address should be related to the learner, their goals, and the person behind the learner. It's obvious that you want to know more about the type of learner you're designing for and what their needs and goals are. At the same time, you want to empathize with the person you're interviewing. What does a day in the life of this person look like? What do they enjoy or dislike? What is their background?

Questions like this can help paint a better and more detailed picture of the learner. I once interviewed a student in Singapore who chose to go to a certain school primarily because it was close to home. I might have assumed he did not want to put in the effort to go farther. Instead, I asked why this was so important. The student replied that as the oldest son in a Malay family he has many obligations and responsibilities at home. He wanted to be there for his family and be able to study. This taught me two things. First, don't judge too quickly. Second, asking follow-up questions makes all the difference.

Focus groups

Gather a group of learners and focus their attention on a topic, question, problem, or outcome. Observing and listening to the group's interactions and discussion can be a great source of information.

Focus groups are often used for developing new consumer products. Participants are asked about the flavor of new cookies, the packaging of detergent, or a company's possible rebranding. When you use focus groups with learners, the same principles apply, but the topic is obviously different.

Focus groups might be less natural than contextual observation, but you have more control over the situation. You can prepare better, as you can plan in advance, and be present to guide the session.

Other than in an interview, you can have group interaction and discussion to enrich the conversation. If one learner answers a question, others will likely respond. When the majority agrees, that's a strong indicator that their opinion will be shared by most learners within the larger target audience. When there is disagreement, you can gather different perspectives on the same matter. This can help in formulating a diversified design strategy in order to do justice to the diversity of the target audience.

Here are some example questions you can ask:

- How do you feel about this topic?
- What do you like or dislike about this topic?
- What kind of experience would you prefer?
- What would be a desirable outcome?
- How will this outcome benefit you in your personal, professional, and/or academic life?

Design

You need ideas to create a design. Being able to generate good ideas will enable you to create great designs and original designs that work.

Generating ideas is a skill, not a talent. You can develop this skill through practice. In fact, learning to generate loads of (good) ideas is a vital part of any design education. Whether you are designing a logo or an experience, it all starts with a good idea.

You need good ideas for great designs. Below I have outlined the general steps that take you from getting ideas to creating a design. Before you get started, I want to point out that anyone can come up with ideas. While some doubt their creative talents, this is something you can do if you are willing to give it a try and keep practicing. Don't be afraid, and just have fun. Persevering will boost your creative confidence.

We'll step through these phases of design:

1. Ideation: Divergence

2. Ideation: Convergence

3. Conceptualization: draft design

4. Detailed design

Also, we'll look at the value of co-creation with learners where that is possible.

1. Ideation: Divergence

Goal: Generate loads of ideas.

Let's start with trying to come up with lots of ideas. At first you don't focus on the quality of the ideas but on the quantity. When aiming for quantity, it helps to not criticize ideas straightaway. Simply let anyone spill out any idea that comes to mind. Write them all down without judgment. You'd be surprised how silly ideas can turn out to be great ideas.

What I've discovered when conducting LXD training is that many people without a design background generally struggle with ideation. There are three pitfalls they tend to fall into:

- Listing existing, generic ideas

- Listing goals or topics instead of ideas

- Modifying an existing idea without improving

To illustrate these pitfalls, I'd like to use the example of creating a learning experience about the benefits of meditation.

Pitfall: Listing existing, generic ideas

This happens a lot; instead of coming up with original ideas, people first think of existing ideas that are generic and not very useful. Here are some examples:

- Play a game

- Watch a video

- Read a book

- Have a conversation

- Use a trainer

- Use blended learning

- Use microlearning

- Use gamification

- Create an app

If you think about using a game, a video, or an app, you must add much more detail to call it an idea. For example:

> I can create a video with a personal message from a friend motivating them to do a couple of easy meditation exercises to get started.

That's an idea that's concrete enough to value and broad enough to work out in more detail.

Pitfall: Listing goals or topics instead of ideas

If the learning experience is about meditation, you might confuse goals with ideas. A list of goals or topics would look like this:

- Learn to relax

- Control breathing

- Learn to sit still

- Lead a healthy lifestyle

- Explore different kinds of meditation

- Guided meditation

- Focused attention

- Body scan

- Mindfulness

Having these suggestions is great for exploring the topic of meditation or formulating a learning outcome or learning objectives. Use them to generate ideas. For example:

> Save time and refresh the mind by doing guided meditation on the train to or from work.

Pitfall: Modifying an existing idea without improving

The third pitfall is a bit tricky. When you take an existing idea and modify it, it can work. The pitfall is to modify it in an unimaginative way.

It's easy to come up with something like Mindful Monopoly. It could be the same format as the game but with different content — perhaps changing street names to mindful exercises. That's not an original idea.

Let's say you want to create Mindful Monopoly properly; you could:

- Consider how to make the game playable and on topic

- Use game elements of Monopoly like buying a street or taking a chance card to create your own game

- Dig deeper into the rules of Monopoly that make it such a timeless game

- Consider: what are different strategies to play Monopoly?

In the end, your game may look nothing like Monopoly, which is probably a good thing.

One brick, a thousand ideas!

Here's a classic exercise to practice generating ideas. Try listing all the ways you can use a brick. Think about it: What can you do with a single brick? Many things!

The brick can be a paperweight, a weapon, a step, a door stop, construction material, and more. You can also come up with all kinds of activities with a brick. Who can throw the brick the farthest? Use it for weight training. Do a relay race with a brick. Try to keep balance while standing on the brick. And so on. If a simple brick sparks so many ideas, anything can.

2. Ideation: Convergence

Goal: Pick the best idea(s).

It's time to choose the ideas that are the most viable. Now it's all about quality and not about quantity. If you end up with one or two great ideas, that's more than enough.

An easy way to pick the best idea in a group is by giving each person points they can award to the different ideas. For example, your favorite will get three points, the next will get two, and the next will get one point. The ideas with the most points (from all participants) are selected.

3. Conceptualization: Draft design

Goal: Determine if your ideas are viable.

A good idea is great, but it is only the beginning. Now your idea needs to evolve into a design. This process is called conceptualization.

You start by creating a draft design. A draft design shows what makes your idea unique and if, how, and why it is going to work. By doing so, it enables you to figure out if you have a viable idea or if you need better ideas.

Your draft design includes key aspects of the learning experience like the overall process, the main activities that take place, the location of the experience, and the resources that you're going to use. It doesn't have to be detailed; it just needs enough detail to communicate your idea effectively. This can be in many forms like of a written document, the outline of a learner journey, a scenario, a sketched storyboard, or a combination of these.

For example, I was asked to come up with an idea to explain the interdependence between time, scope, and budget when managing a project. In short, the idea was to have three groups of people to represent time, scope, and budget, and one group to represent a client. Together they would try to find the best balance for a successful project: a fun idea that could work better than explaining these concepts with a flip chart. When I started conceptualizing this idea, I worked out rules of play, specific challenges, the needs of the client, timing, and so on. All of this was done in writing along with a couple of quick sketches. This was enough to clarify the idea and figure out the next steps of the design.

Adding visuals can help clarify the draft design drastically. A picture can tell a thousand words, and a simple sketch can already make a huge difference. Especially with complex or abstract aspects like interaction or a digital interface. You don't have to create picture perfect visuals to communicate an idea. A simple sketch can be enough.

4. Detailed design

Goal: Create a design that you can share with other people and is ready for development.

It takes several steps to go from your first idea to a final design. Each step makes your design more detailed, refined, and concrete.

A draft design is generally not enough to present to a client or to proceed to the next phase of development. For example, you probably need more detail in your design to turn it into a functioning prototype. If you are working with software developers, they want clear and precise input on what they need to build.

Learning experiences come in many shapes and sizes. Depending on the type of experience you design, conceptualization can take hours, days, or months. Conceptualizing a two-hour workshop is different from planning a year-long playful blended learning experience.

Whatever your experience may be like, you need to be able to share it with other people. You want to create a design that clearly explains what the experience is going to be like. This can be done in various ways. You can create detailed wireframes, a strong look and feel, complete learner journeys, or mockups that simulate an interactive experience. Typically, I combine different forms to share my story effectively.

I've learned that the parts of your design that are visible, like the interface of an app or the board of a board game, have a huge influence on how your design is perceived. It's only natural for people to focus on what they see, while many intricacies of your design aren't always visible.

Let's say you are presenting your design to a client. You've spent a lot of time working on refined structures, clever interactions, a great flow, smart learning strategies, and fun game mechanics, but that's not easy to communicate. What the client sees is what gets them excited. If they like what they see, they are more interested in everything that's going on under the hood. If they don't like what they see, you will have a hard time convincing them.

Creating an appealing design helps you to get people on board. Having strong visuals is inviting and makes things easier to understand. That's why visual design is always an important part of my work.

Having visual design skills is very helpful if not essential here. If that's not (yet) your strength, you can also search for existing graphics, illustrations, pictures, or videos. In time, though, this is a skill that you want to add to your LXD skillset.

Depending on the type of experience you design, you might need other design skills from disciplines like interaction design, user experience design, experience design, or game design. That's why having a design background is beneficial for mastering LXD. Simply put, you need professional design skills to be(come) a learning experience designer.

When your design is ready, it is time for development. This is when you turn your design into a prototype. After testing your prototype, you will iterate your design until you are ready to launch. In each cycle, the design will get closer to its final form.

Before we get into development, let's look at ways to co-create during the design phase.

Co-creation

Involving the learner in the design process is a great way to enhance and enrich your design. Co-creation allows learners to actively work on the learning experience you create. There are several moments in the design process where co-creation works well; here are three examples.

Ideation with learners

Learners participate in a brainstorm session where they come up with their own ideas. They are also invited to bounce other ideas off each other and select the most viable ones. It's like instant user testing when the learner can add and pick ideas that work for them. Remember that not everyone feels confident enough to simply start spilling ideas. Ensure there is a safe environment where no idea is a bad idea and everyone feels free to share what they think.

Conceptualization with learners

Get learners involved in working out the best ideas in more detail. Where an idea can be broad or vague, a concept is more detailed. During this step, you start to think about how, where, and when the learning experience is going to take place. Many questions will arise about what is or isn't going to work in the real world. Having the learner there to think about these questions is a great asset.

Prototyping with learners

When your design is made tangible, it's easier to see how and if it's going to work. Having learners co-create prototypes makes the process more focused on the needs of the learner. They might see opportunities or spot problems you overlooked. When you prototype, you're not just developing exactly what you designed. It's also a creative process in which solutions can be found for challenges that arise. You can easily adjust things on the fly and do quick tests of your prototype.

Develop

You have created your design. Now it's time to breathe life into it and enter the development phase.

Developing a learning experience takes place in iterations. It starts with a first prototype and ends with a finalized learning experience that's ready to launch. Learning experiences can take many shapes and forms, and development is just as versatile. This means you might have to learn to use new tools or software.

For example, a client asked me to use specific e-learning authoring software I had never used before. I decided to learn on the job, and that worked out well. Sometimes things can get a lot more complicated. For example, when my team and I designed a blended learning platform, we couldn't develop it ourselves. It required the help of specialized developers. Developers I work with have an affinity with design just as I have an affinity with development. Mutual respect and a shared understanding are the foundation of creating learning experiences that look, function, and feel good.

I do believe that a designer should be able to build stuff themselves for two reasons. One is to fully understand the design process. When you've gone through every step of the process by yourself, you will discover what works and what doesn't. After that, when you work with developers, you'll be able to empathize with them and create designs that are unique and realistic.

The second reason is because being a learning experience designer often requires you to quickly turn your ideas into reality. Being able to develop things yourself adds a lot of value to the work that you do. The more tangible your design is, the easier it is to get your learners and your client on board.

No matter what kind of learning experience you develop, it starts with a prototype. I'd like to focus on prototyping as part of development because it is an indispensable skill for any learning experience designer.

Prototyping

Prototyping is a fun and challenging part of the design process. There are different ways to develop a prototype. The method of prototyping you choose depends on the type of experience that you've designed.

For example, an experience with a board game would need to have the actual game prototyped. You can keep this simple in its appearance, but all the elements must be usable. An online learning experience requires a prototype of the digital user interface. This can be done either on paper or digitally. Whether the prototype is more of a rough sketch or already close to the final experience depends on what you're trying to achieve with the prototype.

As you can see, there are a lot of options to choose from. The first choice you must make is between a mock-up and a functional prototype.

A mock-up is quicker to create but offers a less realistic experience. A functional prototype may take more time to develop, but it will offer a more realistic experience.

What you choose depends on how close you are to finalizing your design. A design process takes several iterations. For each iteration, the proto-type will come closer to the final design. You want to start with a rapid prototype at first. This makes the experience more tangible, which makes numerous design choices a lot easier. If you create only one prototype that's already close to final, you miss out on so many opportunities to learn and to fine-tune your design.

Some people don't prototype at all. This might work if you create learning experiences that are like ones you've created before. I've met e-learning designers who said that 90% of their e-learning modules are identical; only the content changes, and an extra exercise might be added. In that case, prototyping doesn't add much value. When you design a unique experience that's never been done before, you need prototypes to test your assumptions and challenge your design choices.

Often a learning experience consists of different activities. Each of these activities might require a different prototype. For example, one activity could be virtual and another one a group exercise. You can imagine the prototypes for these activities are vastly different. Besides these proto-typed activities, you also want to prototype the overall experience. The easiest way to do that is by describing what happens before, in between, and after the activities.

Of course, you can also prototype the complete experience from start to finish, but that's not always realistic. Try to focus on the parts of the experience that are crucial to its success first. Once those key moments are done, you can move on to the rest of the experience.

Rapid prototyping

The easiest and fastest way to prototype your design is on paper. Developing a paper prototype is something anybody can do, and it can really benefit your design process without investing a lot of time or money.

This section shares how to create your own paper prototype. Don't worry, you don't have to be an artist to create a paper prototype. Anybody can do it! You just have to try it and not be afraid to fail. Because paper prototyping is fast you can easily redo (part of) your prototype.

What do you need?

You don't need very much for this type of prototype other than a draft design based on a good idea. In terms of physical materials, you need just a few sheets of paper and something to draw with, preferably a marker, but a pen or pencil will do.

Most essential, you need people who will test your prototype — we'll call them the *test group*. Ideally, they should be similar to the people you actually design for, but they don't have to be. Testing early and often is more important than doing one perfect test.

How do you start?

A first step is to look at the resources that are going to be used in your learning experience. For example, your learners might use a phone or playing cards or watch a video in your design.

Next, you want to look at what else your users would need besides the resources to experience your design, such as instructions or an assignment.

Are we done?

Maybe you need to add more detail or variations of your resources, such as different screens in an app that simulate interaction.

Now it's time to test, right?

Absolutely. It's as simple as that! You can guide your test group through the experience using the materials you've created. You'll learn more about testing in just a moment!

What if the design fails completely?

Great job! You've just learned a lot about what may or may not work, especially what doesn't work. All you need is another 15 to 30 minutes to change your design and create a new prototype.

What if everything works perfectly?

Congrats, you can now continue to develop and refine the prototype toward a learning experience that can be launched.

Tips for development

Development encompasses a broad spectrum of activities and skills. Going from the first prototype to the final experience isn't a straightforward process. Sometimes you're able to develop the whole experience by yourself. In other cases, you might need a complete team of developers to turn your innovative design into an incredible experience. Whatever may be the case, here are some tips that basically apply to any situation:

- Start prototyping as soon as possible.

- You can prototype vital parts of the experience first.

- Prototype often, as each iteration will improve the quality of your design.

- Choose the right level of detail, keeping your prototype as simple as possible to save time and money.

- Invite developers to join the design process from start to finish. This will help with the development of the prototypes and the final design.

- Enjoy the process of experimentation and creation as a source of inspiration and wonder.

 # Test

There's only one way to find out if your design works: test it! Test it frequently for the best results.

Testing experiences is common practice in user experience design (UXD). You can design a user experience with the best intentions in the world only to find out the user is lost and having a terrible experience. That's why it's of vital importance to test your design thoroughly and improve as much as you can before you launch.

The same applies to LXD. You want to ensure the learner reaches all learning objectives and achieves the desired learning outcome in a positive, personal, and profound way. You want the learner to have a great experience.

Many of the testing methods used in UXD also work for LXD. These methods range from quick and simple to elaborate scientific testing. How you choose to test your design depends on the type of experience you've created and what is expected from the learner.

For example, you might work on a casual learning experience for kids at home that uses short stories that include fun facts about nature. Testing if kids like the stories is quite straightforward. You simply let them read the stories, see how they react, and chat about what they liked and disliked. When you add a few questions at the end to see if they remember most of the fun facts, you are basically done.

What happens when you have designed a game for chemistry students who are preparing to graduate? The stakes are higher, and the experience requires a more sophisticated prototype. When you test a game, it must be playable. This is often a challenge. When you play a game where the rules are unclear or the game mechanics are unbalanced, it is not any fun. Also, both digital and board games can take a long time to prototype with stuff to be printed or programmed.

Once you have a prototype that works, you still need to ensure the students reach the desired learning outcome. As the consequences of not reaching the outcome are serious, you would need to test extensively and preferably using a structured scientific approach.

As you can see from these two examples, testing can range from simple and quick to complex and time-consuming. There is no standard for testing learning experiences. For each experience you will have to come up with tests that are specific to the kind of experience you've designed.

Frequent testing pays off

A quick word of advice on testing: It's better to do fast and frequent tests than one big test at the end.

I always enjoy sharing a first paper prototype with the learner to see their reaction. This can really boost your design process with loads of valuable feedback.

When you do one big user test, you will be left with many new questions you want answered, because a test doesn't just provide answers; it raises just as many questions. You might not have the time and resources to improve your design when you're at the end of your project.

Now I will give you an example of testing we did when we developed a computer game for school kids aged 8 to 12. The first testing was done using a paper prototype to see if they liked our ideas, including the game concept, character design, and visual design. It was a proof of concept and gave us the assurance that we were on the right track.

Our game concept used several worlds with mini games hidden in them. Obviously, each world and mini game was individually tested frequently by people in and around the office. It's too time-consuming to arrange tests with students all the time, and since the students liked the concept of the game, we decided to continue testing it ourselves. Once the mini games worked well, we tested the complete game with the learners. Overall, they liked what they saw, and with some final adjustments the game was done.

Launch

Your design is tested and ready to be launched! What could go possibly wrong? Well ...

There is a big difference between testing a design and having your design being used for real. Once you have launched your design, it is out of your hands, and you can expect the unexpected:

- Less control over the actual experience

- Larger scale, which can lead to bigger problems

- Different people having different experiences

Control

When you test a design, you are operating in a relatively controlled environment. Most of the time the person who conducts the test is present. They can offer support and guidance to the learner, address problems as they arise, and empathize with the learner when things go wrong.

This is not the case when you've launched. For example, you do not have control over the environment around the learner — physical or technological. You won't be there to fix problems when they occur or react to unexpected events. That's why user testing is necessary before you launch.

Scale

When scale increases, you can also expect an increase in problems. More people will participate in your learning experience, and each of these people can act or react differently.

Problems can occur more often, or new problems can arise such as technical difficulties, questions from learners, or limited bandwidth.

I was part of a project where we designed an experience that included a board game. The design was tested and improved several times, and we hurried to get everything to the printer. When we received the printed games, it turned out that there were some small mistakes. Those could be fixed with some added stickers, but it would have been better to prevent the mistakes from happening.

Prepare to launch

How can you prevent problems from occurring in the first place? It's all about the design process and the care and attention that you give to the learner and the experience you design for. If you understand the people who you design for, where they come from, and in which environment they learn, you kind of know what to expect.

A design is not a finished product. It is work in progress, and it requires several attempts to get it right. Do your research, refine the outcome, care for the learner, push your creative boundaries, prototype, test and iterate your design, and learn from your mistakes so you can launch a learning experience that does the job and gets people excited.

Once you are confident that your learning experience is ready to be released to the world, it's time to plan a spectacular launch.

3, 2, 1, Launch!

There are many ways to launch a learning experience. It can be as simple as pushing a button, or you can take it many steps further and throw a launch party.

Let's say you've designed an e-learning module for a company that's ready to launch. You can press Publish in a learning management system and that's it. Or you can generate a buzz and get people excited first. Send out an intriguing announcement that sparks curiosity. Get people talking and ready to learn. Set a launch date and organize an event to mark the occasion. When you launch, it is a celebration of the effort of everyone involved. It should highlight what it will bring to the learner and the company.

Each step of the design process is vital. Not thinking or caring about how you launch your learning experience is a shame. The launch of a learning experience is already part of the experience itself. Treat it that way and design an activity to kick off the learning experience spectacularly.

What tools can help you through this process?

It's one thing to sketch out the stages of a design process, which will be familiar to those of you from a design background. However, for LXD there is a specific tool that I have designed that we will cover next in Chapter 6, "The Learning Experience Canvas." Then in Chapter 7, "Design Tools," we will look at how some other methods and practices can support the LXD process.

It's so fine and yet so terrible to stand in front of a blank canvas.

—PAUL CÉZANNE, ARTIST

Chapter 6

GET THE MOST OUT OF
The Learning Experience Canvas

Design is an applied form of art. Just like an artist, designers need a canvas to work with. Starting with an empty canvas unlocks creative energy and allows you to create unique designs.

After learning about the designer and the design process, it's time to focus on the tools you use as a learning experience (LX) designer (**FIGURE 6.1**). The Learning Experience Canvas (LX Canvas) is the first, and most important, tool that I will introduce in this book.

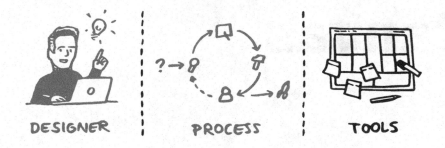

FIGURE 6.1 *Now we move from the designer and process to focus on your tools.*

This chapter is exclusively about the LX Canvas. In the next chapter you will find other useful tools that complement your design skills and process.

Download the LX Canvas

Before you continue reading, make sure you have downloaded and preferably printed the LX Canvas. Simply visit **www.lxcanvas.com** to register and download the LX Canvas for free.

Introducing the LX Canvas

When you look at all the elements that come into play when you design a learning experience, things can get a bit overwhelming and sometimes confusing. That's why I felt the need for a tool to make things a bit easier and ultimately to improve each part of the design process. So, I created the LX Canvas.

At first, it was a tool my team and I used for projects. Soon people in my professional network started asking if they could use it as well. That's when I decided to make it available online for free. Over the years, as downloads started to increase, many thousands of people from all over the world have downloaded it. It's not a software application — it's a structured document provided as a PDF (**FIGURE 6.2**).

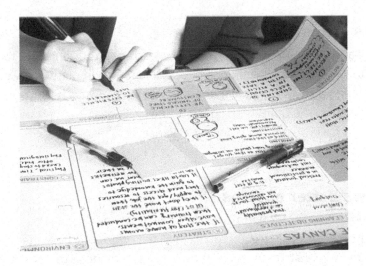

FIGURE 6.2 *The LX Canvas in use. (Photo by Niels Floor)*

How the LX Canvas supports the design process

Based on my own experience and on responses from the learning experience design (LXD) community, I've identified five attributes of the LX Canvas that make a difference.

Helps you structure your design

Every learning experience consists of the elements that are featured on the LX Canvas. These elements are structured in a way to support your design and your design process. Use the LX Canvas throughout the design process to create designs that are well-thought-out, original, and memorable.

This chapter covers each element individually in a sensible order. To get started, you can easily follow that order when using the LX Canvas. Once you get familiar with the LX Canvas, you can use it more dynamically. It's not a step-by-step exercise but a tool made to enhance creativity and effectiveness.

Gives a clear overview

There's a lot going on when you design a learning experience. It's too much to keep track of if you don't have a clear and complete overview. But creating an overview is not enough; you must always be sure you are staying true to the goals of the design. The LX Canvas shows you and the entire team all you need to know, at a glance, at all times.

Allows better choices

With the right structure and a clear overview, it's much easier to make the right choices for your design. You have all the information you need in one place, and with a structured workflow it's easy to choose the best option for your learning experience.

Easy to use

The LX Canvas is an easy tool to use. You can simply print it, and all you need to get started is a pencil and possibly some sticky notes. You can even quickly re-create the LX Canvas on a piece of paper or flip chart if you don't have a printer or want to scale up. A larger scale makes using it in a group, which I recommend, more effective as everyone can see what's happening and contribute to the session.

Versatile

It doesn't matter what type of learning experience you want to design; the LX Canvas is universally applicable. I've used the LX Canvas for all kinds of clients with completely different projects ranging from a couple of hours to months or years. The LX Canvas is truly versatile, and I'm confident it will work just as well for you.

In fact, the LX Canvas can also be used in other ways for other purposes. For instance, it's a great tool for analyzing existing learning experiences when you are redesigning a learning experience.

Structure of the LX Canvas

There is a clear intention behind the way the LX Canvas is structured.

From the moment I created the LX Canvas in 2013 up until now, I've had many questions on why it looks exactly the way it does. Could there be something that's missing? Is there a better structure? Does it work for all learning experiences?

I've always listened carefully to any questions or criticism and looked closely if the LX Canvas needed changes. So far, I've concluded that it works as intended and there's no need for change. Let me explain the ideas behind the way the LX Canvas is structured (**FIGURE 6.3**).

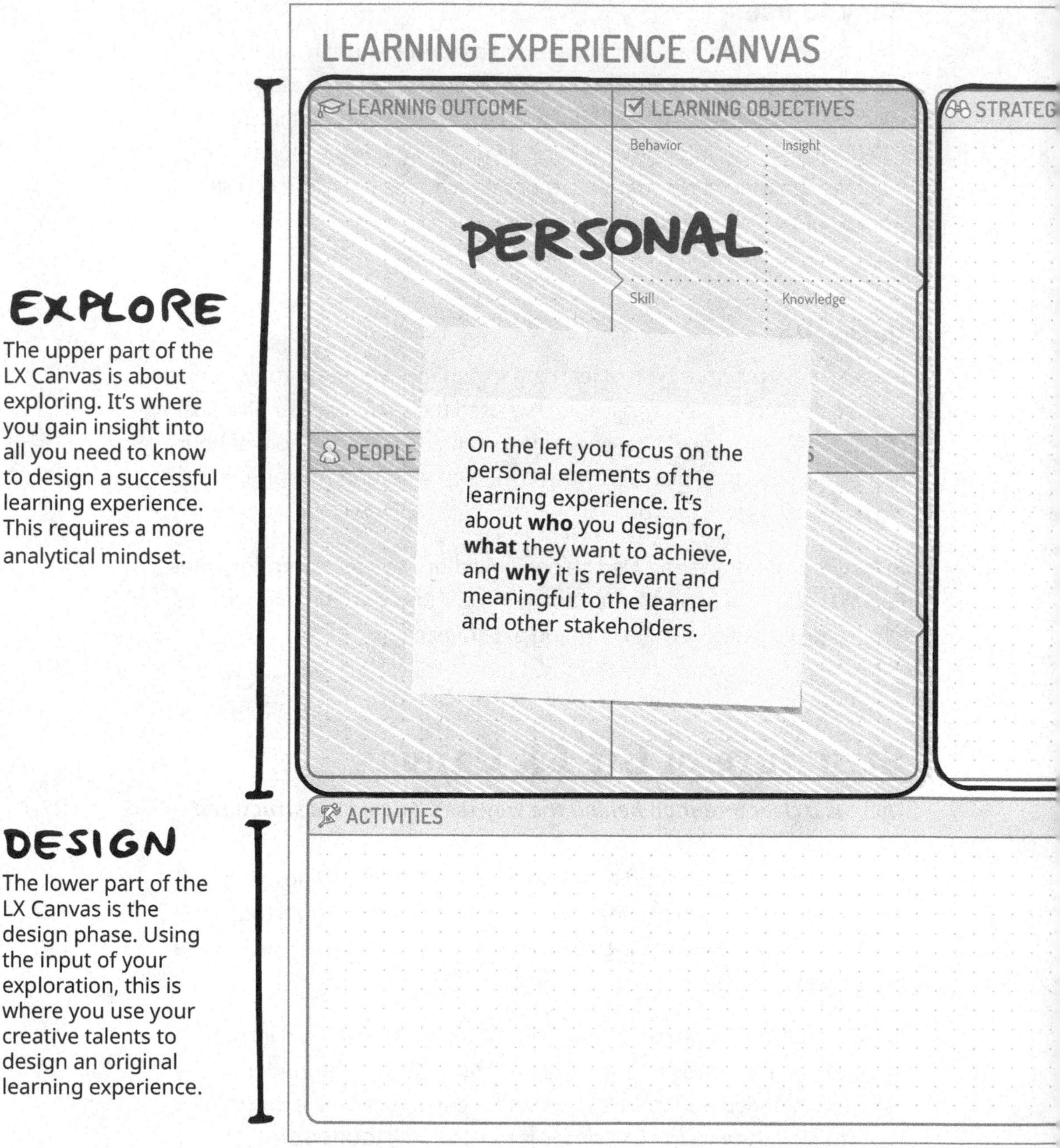

LEARNING EXPERIENCE CANVAS

LEARNING OUTCOME   ✓ LEARNING OBJECTIVES   👓 STRATEG

Behavior   Insight

PERSONAL

Skill   Knowledge

👤 PEOPLE

On the left you focus on the personal elements of the learning experience. It's about **who** you design for, **what** they want to achieve, and **why** it is relevant and meaningful to the learner and other stakeholders.

EXPLORE

The upper part of the LX Canvas is about exploring. It's where you gain insight into all you need to know to design a successful learning experience. This requires a more analytical mindset.

🏃 ACTIVITIES

DESIGN

The lower part of the LX Canvas is the design phase. Using the input of your exploration, this is where you use your creative talents to design an original learning experience.

FIGURE 6.3 *The two phases within the Learning Design Canvas.*

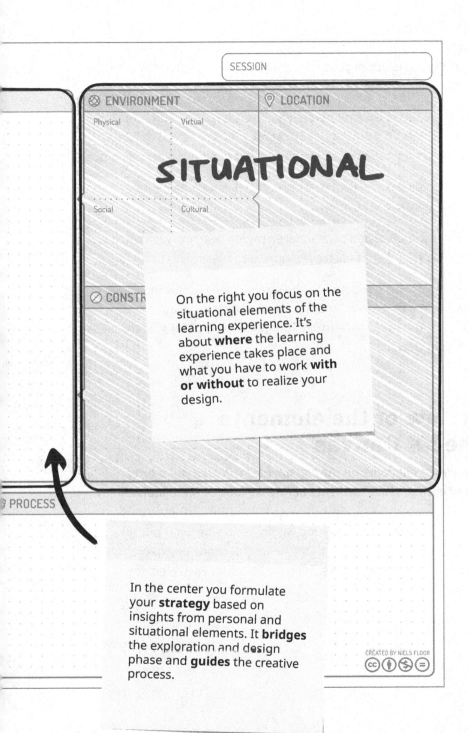

SESSION

ENVIRONMENT

Physical   Virtual

SITUATIONAL

Social   Cultural

LOCATION

CONSTR

On the right you focus on the situational elements of the learning experience. It's about **where** the learning experience takes place and what you have to work **with or without** to realize your design.

PROCESS

In the center you formulate your **strategy** based on insights from personal and situational elements. It **bridges** the exploration and design phase and **guides** the creative process.

The LX Canvas is divided into two phases. The first is exploration, and the second is design. The upper part is for exploring, and the lower part is for your design.

Obviously, you need to explore before you design. Your design is based on the lessons learned from your exploration. It prepares you to focus your creativity on finding original solutions and creating unique designs.

The exploration part consists of three groups: personal elements, situational elements, and strategy.

In essence, the personal and situational elements describe who you design for, what they want to achieve, and where everything takes place.

All these elements come together in the strategy. The flow is indicated with arrows on the LX Canvas. You work toward a strategy as you complete and refine the personal and situational elements. The strategy leads to creating your design.

Overview of the elements on the LX Canvas

There are eleven elements on the LX Canvas. I will give you a brief overview of each of these elements before we look at them individually.

This overview is always handy to keep within reach when you design a learning experience. We begin with the various sections of exploration, starting with the personal factors. Then we'll explore each element more deeply.

Learning outcome

Describe what the learner will gain from the learning experience and why that's meaningful and valuable to the learner.

The main questions are:

- What does the learner gain from this experience?

- Why is this the desired result, and how is it relevant for the learner?

- How does this affect the learner on a personal, professional, and/or academic level?

Learning objectives

List the specific goals that the learner needs to reach to achieve the desired learning outcome. There are four kinds of objectives: insight, knowledge, skills, and behavior.

The main questions are:

- What are the different types of learning objectives that the learner wants to reach?

- Will reaching those learning objectives enable the learner to achieve the desired learning outcome?

People

List all groups of people who either participate in the learning experience or who have a stake in the learning experience. Some learners may already be grouped, such as people from a place or a company. Or you may identify a group such as those who share a profession or role.

The main questions are:

- Who is taking part in this learning experience?

- What are the primary and secondary groups who participate?

- What other stakeholders are part of this experience?

Characteristics

Describe the people who are part of your learning experience in a more detailed way, offering insights into who they are.

The main questions are:

- What is characteristic for the people in this learning experience?

- What are their views, talents, limitations, interests, or other relevant attributes?

- What makes them different or unique?

- What do they have in common?

Location

Defining where the learning experience will take place is the first of the four situational factors. For example, it might be a space or a building in a particular city. There can be one or more locations, or it could be virtual, accessible from anywhere.

The main questions are:

- Where is the experience taking place exactly?

- What options do we have to choose from for picking the right location?

- Will it be in one or more than one location?

Environment

Describe how people will interact with each other and their surroundings in the location or locations of the learning experience. It's important to think about how we are affected by the environment in which we learn.

The main questions are:

- How do we interact with each other in this environment?

- In what way does the environment enable or disable learning?

- Is this location right for this learning experience?

Resources

Describe everything you have at your disposal for the creation and implementation of your learning experience.

The main questions are:

- What resources are at our disposal?
- How can we best use the available resources?

Constraints

Include all the limitations to the design, realization, and implementation of a learning experience.

The main questions are:

- What are the (main) limitations that affect this learning experience?
- How do they affect the learning experience?
- Can we work around these limitations?

Strategy

This is a separate section within the exploration phase comprising a set of design guidelines. These should be based on the analysis of the personal and situational elements on the LX Canvas.

The main questions are:

- What correlations between different elements of the LX Canvas can we find?

- Are the different elements aligned or contradictory?

- What design guidelines can we formulate based on what is written on the LX Canvas?

Activities

Now we've entered the design phase and need to describe what the learner actually does during the learning experience. An activity enables the learner to reach one or more learning objectives.

The main questions are:

- What are the people who take part in the experience going to do?

- What learning objectives will each activity achieve?

- When all activities are completed, will the desired learning outcome be achieved?

Process

The final element of the LX Canvas should describe the actual learning experience as it takes place over time. It is an arranged and scheduled set of activities.

The main questions are:

- When will the learning experience that you've designed take place?

- In what order, for how long, and at what time will activities take place?

- What will the complete learning experience look like for the learner; what is the learner journey?

- How will the learner feel throughout the process?

Learning outcome

A learning outcome describes the actual result the learner gains from a learning experience.

Having a well-crafted learning outcome will give meaning, purpose, and direction to the design of the learning experience and to the actual learning experience itself.

It is highly recommended that you formulate the learning outcome in the beginning of your design process. This will enable you to start with the end in mind. In other words, you'll have a clear vision of where you want to end up with your design.

Once you have the learning outcome clearly formulated, everything you do is pointed in that direction. You are continually working toward the desired learning outcome. Each decision you make during the design process is made with the intention to come closer to achieving the goals of the learner.

What does the learner gain from this experience?

The learning outcome should explain to the learner what they are going to get out of the experience that you've designed.

Formulating learning outcomes is a common practice in education, but we are going to define learning outcomes differently. Often a learning outcome is formulated as a goal. For example, at the end of the class, you will have learned to multiply numbers. This looks like a well-formulated learning outcome, but it is only a learning objective.

Often learning objectives and learning outcomes are used as identical or interchangeable terms. There is a big difference, though. Let me explain this using an analogy.

Let's imagine you want to build a house. You'd have to set and reach several goals to design and build the house. Once you complete the house and you start living there, the house becomes a home. It offers shelter, safety, and comfort. It is a place where you make memories and feel at ease. If building a house is the learning objective, feeling at home is the learning outcome.

Why is this the desired result, and how is it relevant for the learner?

A good learning outcome makes perfect sense to the learner. The best way to put your learning outcome to the test is to see how the learners react to reading the learning outcome. Are they excited to learn? Or are they not that inspired or even demotivated to learn?

When you write a learning outcome, you want to clarify to the learner why this outcome is relevant and meaningful to them. It's obvious that an irrelevant and meaningless outcome has no value to the learner. This is basically a waste of their time: They won't be motivated to learn, as they are not interested in what they might gain from the experience.

How does this affect the learner on a personal, professional, and/or academic level?

What you learn can benefit you in different areas of your life. In my experience, people tend to limit these benefits to the context the experience is designed for. For example, a corporate time management training is designed only to benefit the working life of the learner. Often there are benefits that surpass that one area. What you apply in business may also be applicable in your private life. Mastering time management can work just as well at home or for your academic development. It may help you to find more time to spend with your kids or study more effectively. Making clear to the learner how one thing you learn can help you in different parts of life adds value and increases motivation to learn.

How to write an effective learning outcome

Two steps can help with writing an effective learning outcome: First, create a mind map, and then build the story. Key points and an example will help you master this vital skill.

Step 1: Mind map

Creating a mind map is a simple and effective way to start exploring possible learning outcomes. Take a large sheet of paper and write down the theme or subject of your learning experience in the center, such as "communication skills." Draw a circle around the words "communication skills." Now start writing down any benefits that you associate with communication skills or situations where these skills can be of value (**FIGURE 6.4**).

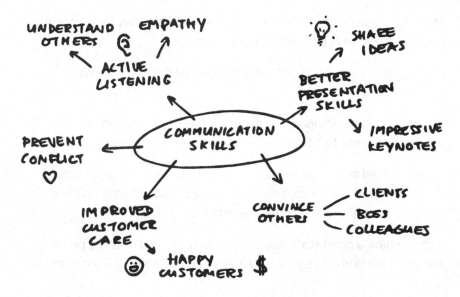

FIGURE 6.4 *An example of a mind map.*

Once you have a full sheet of paper, it's time to categorize. I like to categorize in terms of primary and secondary benefits based on what has the highest value. Also, you can look at whether a benefit applies to the personal, professional, or academic development of the learner.

Step 2: Story

The mind map that you've just created is a great inspiration for writing the learning outcome. Take the most important benefit from the mind map as a starting point for a particular kind of user story.

The biggest pitfall in writing a learning outcome is to write from the perspective of the expert. You want to write from the perspective of the learner.

Also, you want to try to make a personal connection to the learner. Understanding their emotions and adding an emotional layer to the learning outcome can help achieve this. That's why I'd like you to start with writing:

I am (emotion) about (benefit).

The "I" is the learner, and the emotion describes how they feel about the benefit that you selected. Here's an example:

> "I am excited about the fact that I can get my message across more easily."

Now think about how this would benefit the learner in different parts of their life. Add these benefits in a second line and turn it into a short story:

> "I am excited about the fact that I can get my message across more easily. At work I feel heard and appreciated, and at home I enjoy better conversations and less conflict with my family."

Once you have a good start, you can add another two or three primary benefits in the form of sentences. What you end up with is a short story like this:

> "I am excited about the fact that I can get my message across more easily. At work and at home I feel heard and valued. Being a better listener has helped me to gain a deeper understanding of the people I care about. Colleagues, friends, and family appreciate the conversations we have, and I enjoy sharing my thoughts and feedback with them."

Once you have a draft version of your learning outcome, don't be afraid to share it with other people; feedback from learners can improve your final learning outcome.

Key points

When writing a learning outcome, keep in mind:

- Write from the perspective of the learner, not the perspective of the expert.
- Use language that makes sense to the learner and limit the use of jargon.
- Tell how this learning experience has value to the learner.
- Talk about the benefits, not the goals themselves.

Example learning outcome

Writing an effective learning outcome is not easy. That's why I'd like to share an example with you.

Let's say you want to formulate a learning outcome for running a marathon. At first you might think a proper learning outcome would be as follows:

"I am able to run 42 kilometers within four hours."

This is indeed a clearly formulated goal. However, this is not how a motivating learning outcome should be written. A learning outcome refers to the higher purpose of running this marathon for the runner.

Let's rewrite the learning outcome to show the value of the learning experience to the runner:

> "I am amazed because I thought that running a marathon was something I'd never be able to do, but I did! When I crossed the finish line, I was incredibly proud of myself. I will use this unforgettable experience to overcome fears and obstacles later in life. The healthy lifestyle I developed during the marathon training will become an integral part of my life for years to come."

These are two completely different learning outcomes. Obviously, the second one is more inspiring and motivating. When you start writing a learning outcome, try to think of crossing the finish line and how that will make you feel.

Learning objectives
Learning objectives are the specific goals that the learner needs to reach to achieve the desired learning outcome.

It's important to keep in mind the differences between a learning objective and a learning outcome. These terms are often used interchangeably, but we've seen that they are fundamentally different.

Let's get back to the example of running a marathon. If you want to be able to run a marathon, there are many things you need to learn. You can't just start running. You need the proper technique, nutrition, gear, attitude, and lifestyle. This suggests a multitude of learning objectives such as being able to prepare meals based on nutritional needs or setting up and sticking to your personal training schedule. Only when you achieve all your learning objectives will you be able to run your first marathon (outcome).

The impact of going through the learning experience of training for and completing that first marathon is captured in the learning outcome. As described, this can be a life-changing event that will have a lasting positive impact. A learning outcome describes how the life of a learner will change. A learning objective is a step toward reaching that outcome.

LXD is goal-oriented. Focusing on reaching goals helps learners in their development. Whether or not learning objectives contribute to a positive outcome depends on the goals you set.

Four types of learning objectives

I identify four types of learning objectives: insight, knowledge, skill, and behavior. These four types are based on how we learn from what we experience, as shown in **FIGURE 6.5** and described in Chapter 4, "Experiential learning."

It's important to know these types before you start to define learning objectives for your learning experience.

Each type is described and has a set of verbs that you can use to formulate learning objectives. You can come up with more verbs on your own that fit your project.

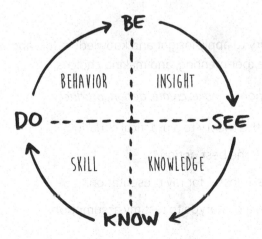

FIGURE 6.5 *Four types of learning objectives.*

Insight

Insight is about observing and reflecting. It is about your perspective and views.

Verbs: *see, notice, recognize, identify, detect, look at, observe.*

> "I see how this subject is relevant to my personal development."

> "I notice how different people have different needs."

> "I recognize the need for a different approach. I look at the problem from a new perspective."

Knowledge

Knowledge is abstract and conceptual. It is about words, facts, data, models, theories, charts, and so on.

Verbs: *know, understand, figure out, find out, grasp.*

> "I know the difference between hamsters and guinea pigs."

> "I understand Newton's third law."

> "I will figure out how to solve this puzzle."

Skill

Skill is the ability to apply insight and knowledge. It is about getting active, doing things, experimenting, and making choices.

Verbs: *apply, choose, make, create, design, produce.*

> "I will apply the theory to a practical situation."

> "I will choose the best option."

> "I will create a poster for my presentation."

> "I will design a prototype to test my assumptions."

Behavior

Behavior is how you incorporate what you've learned in real-life situations. It is about concrete experiences.

Verbs: *be, behave, act, react, live, work.*

> "I will be more disciplined when I'm doing my homework."

> "I will behave less indifferently when a colleague is upset."

> "I will act on the needs of the customers directly and adequately."

> "I will live a more conscious and healthier life."

Learning objectives lead to learning outcome. A learning outcome should be achievable after multiple learning objectives have been reached. So, the key question is: Will reaching these learning objectives enable the learner to achieve the desired learning outcome?

Whether the desired learning outcome is achieved depends on exactly what learning objectives have been reached by the learner. Sometimes there may be learning objectives missing in your design. This problem can arise during a test of the prototype of your design. Maybe a missing insight disables the learner such that they do not fully understand and appreciate new knowledge. Or a missing skill leads to ineffective or unwanted behavior.

Formulating and selecting the learning objectives is like creating a jigsaw puzzle. All the pieces have to fit to get to the desired outcome and see the complete picture. If one or more pieces are missing, you have a problem. Or maybe you have some extra pieces left when the puzzle is already complete. That is less of a problem but still not ideal.

Your challenge is to create all the right pieces of the puzzle. Use all four types of learning objectives to ensure a natural and complete learning experience.

How to formulate learning objectives

Here's an exercise to help you formulate learning objectives.

1. Write a first draft of a learning objective.

Let us continue with the example of running a marathon. This could be a first draft:

> "I need a training schedule for better training."

2. Divide the learning objective into smaller, more specific objectives.

Learning objectives can often be divided into smaller parts. This makes them easier to understand for the learner. It also makes it easier to design the learning experience and to measure the results.

Try to divide each learning objective into the four different types of learning objectives: insight, knowledge, skill, and behavior.

Here are some examples.

> "Training schedules are important." (insight)

> "There's basic knowledge that I need about training schedules." (knowledge)

> "It's a good idea to make my own training schedule." (skill)

> "I need to use the training schedule when I train." (behavior)

3. Choose the right verb for each learning objective.

As mentioned earlier in this chapter, each type of learning objective has its own verbs. Using these verbs makes your learning objectives more active and concrete.

Here are some examples.

"I see how a training schedule is necessary to reach my goals."

"I understand what a training schedule is and how it works."

"I create my own personal training schedule."

"I become a better runner by using my training schedule."

As you can see in **FIGURE 6.6**, learning objectives are preferably short, concrete, active, and measurable.

FIGURE 6.6 *The four types of learning objectives.*

4. Repeat these steps for all learning objectives.

With four different types of learning objectives, you want to ensure all objectives are covered and balanced. You do not want too much knowledge or too few insights, for example.

5. Will these enable the learner to achieve the desired learning outcome?

We end by repeating the key question we discussed earlier. Remember, your goal is always aligned with the goal of the learner: to achieve the desired learning outcome. The only way to get there is through reaching learning objectives. If you feel that the set of learning objectives that you have formulated will enable the learner to get to the learning outcome, that's great. It's time to move on. If not, find out what's missing. And you can always go back and add, change, or remove learning objectives if needed.

People

Include all groups of people who either participate in the learning experience or have a stake in the learning experience.

Learning is about people and their own experiences. As a learning experience designer, you design an experience for people to learn from. There can be many different kinds of people who take part in a learning experience.

Participants

The primary focus is always on the learner. After all, they are the ones who need to learn from the experience you design.

Obviously, other people can also play an important part in a learning experience such as a teacher, trainer, or coach. They can enable, support, or facilitate the process of learning. While their contributions can be essential, the focus on this group is always secondary to the learner.

Less obvious but possibly relevant people may include parents, friends, and family. Anyone in the social environment of the learner can contribute to the experience of the learner. As a parent, you can participate in your child's learning experience. This can deepen and broaden the impact of a learning experience at school.

Stakeholders

Besides the groups of people who actually participate in a learning experience, there are stakeholders.

These stakeholders don't necessarily participate in the learning experience, but they do have a direct or indirect influence on the experience. An important stakeholder is your client. A client can be an individual, a company, or any other kind of organization like a school or nongovernmental organization. When a client pays you to design a learning experience, their stake in the design and the design process is substantial.

Other stakeholders may include subject matter experts, a publisher, or the government. Each of them has a different stake and a different perspective on what the learning experience should be like. And that can be a challenge all in itself.

Part of your job as a learning experience designer is to align the different perspectives and expectations of the participants and stakeholders. These can sometimes be very different or even opposite of each other.

In each case where you have to deal with a number of participants and stakeholders, you want to do two things: First, focus on the learner, and second, make sure all others are satisfied with your design. One way to achieve that is by inviting them to be part of the design process and communicate the importance of human-centered design.

How to list people

FIGURE 6.7 shows a nice way to get an overview of the different types of people who are directly or indirectly part of the learning experience you design.

ACTIVE		PASSIVE
PRIMARY	SECONDARY	STAKEHOLDER

FIGURE 6.7 *All set up to list the people involved with the learning experience.*

The active people are involved in the learning experience. The learner would be in the primary list. If you have different groups of learners, you can list them here. The secondary group includes all people who play an active part in supporting the learner. This includes teachers and trainers or possibly colleagues, friends, or family.

The passive people are stakeholders who do not participate in the learning experience but do have a stake in it. This can be a client, publisher, or investor. Who goes where depends on the situation you're dealing with. If, for example, parents of a student actively support their children as part of the learning experience, they go in the second column. If they are stakeholders but aren't engaged in direct support of this experience, they go in the third column. Clients can also be active secondary participants or passive stakeholders. **FIGURE 6.8** shows an example.

ACTIVE		PASSIVE
PRIMARY	SECONDARY	STAKEHOLDER
CUSTOMER SERVICE EMPLOYEES MANAGEMENT	TRAINER HR DEPARTMENT CEO	CUSTOMERS THE CLIENT

FIGURE 6.8 *Listing participants and stakeholders by role.*

In this example, there is a business that hires you to design a learning experience on customer service. The client is a passive stakeholder. Their goal is to increase profit through better service.

You can see two types of learners, the customer service employees and management. They will be supported by the trainer, the HR department, and their CEO. You want the client to be involved as much as possible to show they care about their learners and are serious about this learning experience. In this case, the CEO is going to be actively involved. This can make a big difference for the learners and the company. Sharing the same experience can contribute to a collaborative, active and supportive culture in the organization. It shows that people on all organizational levels are dedicated to the same learning outcome.

When you fill out this list, think about who goes where and what would happen if they changed roles. In this case, having an engaged CEO can make a big difference for the learner, and it would be a shame not to use this support. Don't see this as set in stone once it's complete. If at any point during the design process it makes sense to add people or change their role, don't hesitate to do so.

Characteristics

Characteristics describe the people who are part of your learning experience in a more detailed way, offering insights into who they are.

Getting to know the learner is achieved through research. Regardless of the method of research you choose, your goal is always the same. You want to get a decent understanding of who the learner is and what they need to achieve a desired learning outcome. That is achieved by connecting with the learner on a cognitive and emotional level. It's a combination of understanding and empathizing. If you want to review research methods, see Chapter 5, "How to design a learning experience."

Knowing your learner isn't the end of this part. There are more people on your list that you want to get to know. Maybe they are not as important as the learner, but still, you should know more about the people who are part of your design. If trainers are vital to your design, you want to support them effectively, and the only way to do that is by doing research. Talk to them to find out what matters to them and why they love what they do.

How to characterize

Look at the different types of people you've written down in the previous step. We're going to look at demographic, cognitive, and personal characteristics. This enables you to list their views, talents, limitations, interests, or other relevant attributes.

Select one group of people, preferably learners.

Start by writing down the basic demographic characteristics that are representative for this group.

- Age (group)
- Gender
- Country and place of residence
- Occupation
- Cultural background

Characteristics such as age, gender, or cultural background can easily evoke prejudice or discrimination. Make sure you treat this respectfully and don't create a stereotypical, racist, or demeaning image.

Now take a closer look at their cognitive characteristics:

- Level of education
- Learning abilities, for instance, attention span, memory, processing speed, and motor skills
- Learning disabilities/difficulties, for instance, dyslexia, ADHD, impaired hearing/vision, or brain damage

Finally, zoom in on the emotional characteristics:

- How does this person feel about learning and about taking part in this learning experience?
- What motivates this person (to learn)?

- What demotivates this person (to learn)?

- What are their passions, such as music, movies, sports, games, cooking, and so on?

Now repeat the first five steps for the other groups of people.

When looking at the people you design for, try to figure out what makes them unique. Also, try to look at what they have in common. Understanding what separates and unites your learners enables you to design experiences that bring people closer together, not despite but because of their differences.

For example, I frequently train people with completely different backgrounds and professions. They may have totally different approaches and views, yet they all share a love for learning and an interest in LXD. I love to bring those people together, offer a shared perspective, and have them learn from each other. This is generally one of the highest-valued parts of the training I provide to international groups.

Once you've gathered data through your design research, it's time to find the best shape or form to present your findings. There are many ways to do that. My two favorites are personas and empathy maps. These will be covered in Chapter 7, "Design tools."

Location

Location is where the learning experience takes place such as a space or a building in a city. There can be one or more locations for a learning experience.

Where you learn impacts how you learn. Choosing a location that enhances a learning experience seems like a logical and obvious choice. However, picking a location is often not a priority and is easily overlooked. For example, a teacher will teach in the classroom that's been appointed by the school. Or a trainer uses the company's training space simply because it's available and familiar.

Often, you do have a choice! This is a valuable insight. You don't always have to choose the default location. Taking a moment to ask yourself if there's a location that could improve the quality and the outcome of the learning experiences is a great starting point. As soon as you start to see the possibilities of using a different location, you'll find all sorts of opportunities to offer a better learning experience. I love to visit a location and let it inspire me.

You may wonder if finding the best location is difficult, time-consuming, and possibly too expensive or simply not achievable. Keep in mind that a location doesn't have to be perfect. It just has to be the best available option. Like any other element of your learning experience, you must remain pragmatic, practical, and imaginative. There are limitations to what's possible, and spending all your money on a superb location is probably not the smart thing to do. Allocating part of your resources for a great location would be a great choice. It's all about balancing the resources and constraints for your learning experience.

When you're a trainer, picking a location can make such a difference. For example, the possibility of going outside can literally add a breath of fresh air. Taking a stroll through nature is a great way to process what you've learned, relax a bit, and revitalize. There are also activities that work better outside than inside. Having a space that feels good and works well for the learner will lift spirits and increase engagement. When you think of the opposite of such a space, it's easy to see the importance of the right location. Imagine being in a dull, uninspired place with bad lighting and uncomfortable furniture. Would you enjoy that experience?

How to pick a location

As I just mentioned, you should have the choice to pick a location instead of having one designated for you. That is the first step.

Second, make a list of the locations that are available to you. These could be spaces in your office, school, or other accessible spaces nearby. Be practical while not leaving out options that might seem less obvious like a park, theater, library, restaurant, or public space.

Next, take a moment to dream about the perfect location. It can be anywhere in the world, so don't limit yourself! A famous theater, historic building, exotic country, or any special place you can come up with.

Now you have a spectrum of options to choose from. In some cases, the ideal spot is attainable. If going to Nepal and seeing Mount Everest is vital to your design and you have the resources, do it! Most of the time we must settle for a good or great option that isn't perfect.

Selecting the best location from your list should revolve around who the learner is, what their goals are, and how this location will serve that purpose. Simply list pros and cons to the locations that you deem most suitable.

Remember that things can change as the design process progresses. Maybe goals change or you discover more about the preferences of the learner and you want to pick a different location. Or someone offers a location to you that wasn't an option before. Either way, keep an open mind toward the location you choose until you finalize the design.

To review:

1. Volunteer to pick the location.

2. Make a list of possibilities.

3. Dream up a perfect location.

4. List pros and cons, revolving around learner needs.

5. Be open to changing location if things change.

Virtual location

What is the location if you design a virtual learning experience? The location is always physical, even with a virtual learning experience. For example, when you log in to do an e-learning module, you might be sitting behind your desk in the office. In that case, the location is the office. Any virtual learning experience has real people who are in the real world; that's the location of the learning experience. The virtual aspect is part of the environment, which will be discussed in the next part.

Example location choice

When I taught LXD at a university, I was always assigned a classroom to teach in. I didn't let that limit how I would teach my students about experiential learning. I took them outside where we used chalk to write and draw on the streets instead of the blackboard. This made them interact with the learning objectives in a physical and fun way.

Going outside is an easy way to get students active and engaged. It's also nice to get out of the classroom and breathe in some fresh air. As we all know, the brain needs oxygen. The air in a classroom always contains less oxygen than outdoor air.

This is a simple example of picking a good spot to learn and teach. When I organize my LXD conference, I tend to work with universities and the spaces they have available. Walking around those spaces and seeing what's possible allows you to come up with activities that fit the spaces perfectly. This back-and-forth process of creating a design, looking at the location, and iterating your design is a great way to get the most out of the location and the overall experience.

Environment

Environment describes how people interact with each other and their surroundings in the locations of the learning experience.

People behave differently in different environments. There could be several reasons for their behavior. Something as simple as the type of furniture you choose can already change things dramatically.

Imagine a traditional classroom with tables and chairs all aligned to face the front of the room. Now replace the furniture with large pillows, bean bags, and sofas arranged in small groups. It's easy to see how this would invite different behavior and change the way students learn dramatically. One is not better than the other; it just depends on what you want to achieve in an environment.

Furniture is part of the physical environment. When you change things in the physical environment, the changes are clear to see. There are also aspects of an environment that are less easy to spot but that we are all aware of: the social and cultural environment.

You could have the same class being taught in two different schools. If one school is traditional and formal and the other is progressive and informal, you would end up with two very different learning experiences. There are rules, sometimes unwritten, that we are aware of and that influence how we behave, what we do, and how we learn. We've all been to places where we didn't feel at ease. It could be a dress code we didn't really understand well, a certain custom or ritual that we didn't know about, or unwritten rules that we weren't aware of. Understanding these rules is essential to delivering a suitable learning experience within a specific environment.

The social and cultural rules that apply to a physical environment also apply to a virtual environment. Learning can take place just as easily in online environments. Within these environments people also interact with each other, but not every virtual environment is the same. Let's say you use social media for learning. The experience on Facebook would be very different from the experience on LinkedIn. Both social media platforms have their own customs and rules.

How to analyze the environment

Four aspects of the learning environment are distinguished on the LX Canvas.

Physical

This concerns all things in the learning environment that the learner can physically touch, such as chairs, desks, whiteboards, and materials, and how these elements influence the learning experience.

Virtual

This concerns the visual and auditive components of a virtual learning environment, such as interface, graphics, narratives, audio effects, and structure, and how the learner interacts with these aspects.

Social

This is about how people interact with each other in an environment. For example, is there a friendly collaborative or harsh competitive atmosphere? Do people socialize, or are they more on their own? In other words, how do people treat each other?

Cultural

This concerns looking at what culture is dominant in an environment. For example, there are organizations with a traditional, formal, and hierarchical culture, and there are more progressive, informal, and flat organizations. It's about the written and unwritten rules that influence our collective behavior.

You are going to re-create the "environment" part of the LX Canvas. Take a large sheet of paper and divide it into four equal parts. Now add the words *physical*, *virtual*, *social*, and *cultural* starting at the upper-left corner and moving clockwise. On your sheet of paper, fill out the data you've gathered on the different elements of the environment you've selected.

As an example, let me tell you about when I conducted the same one-hour training in São Paulo, Brazil, and Utrecht, the Netherlands. On the surface there are many similarities, but the experience for me and the participants was totally different.

In São Paulo, I was standing in front of 80 people in a tall, modern business building. At the same time there were more than 100 people watching online who also participated. Generally, Brazilians are quite laid back, and I was blown away by their incredible energy. As soon as they got their assignments, the whole space became lively and loud. Having a microphone was essential to make myself heard in the space and online. South Americans are known for their enthusiasm, and this was palpable. We wrapped up the day with a rooftop party, which goes to show how they balance work with enjoying a fun and easygoing lifestyle. See **FIGURE 6.9** for my notes on the environment.

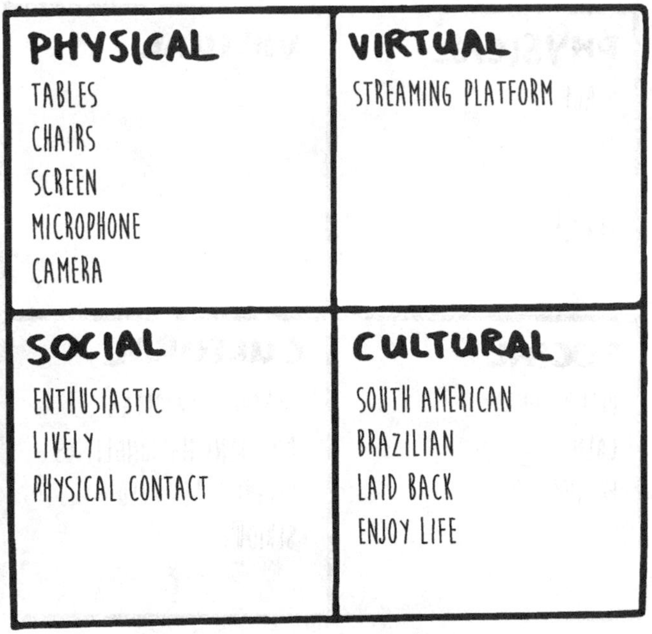

PHYSICAL	VIRTUAL
TABLES CHAIRS SCREEN MICROPHONE CAMERA	STREAMING PLATFORM
SOCIAL	CULTURAL
ENTHUSIASTIC LIVELY PHYSICAL CONTACT	SOUTH AMERICAN BRAZILIAN LAID BACK ENJOY LIFE

FIGURE 6.9 *One-hour training in São Paulo.*

In Utrecht I trained 16 educators from Finland, Belgium, and the Netherlands inside a historic Dutch building. There was no virtual environment. Compared to the situation in São Paulo, it was more serene and formal from the start. While all participants were from Northern Europe, there were clear cultural differences (**FIGURE 6.10**). The Dutch participants took the lead in their groups as people in the Netherlands are quite straightforward. The Belgian participants were more subtle, and they asked many questions. Near the end of the training the Finnish participants shared their observations, solutions, and conclusions. They had mostly been quiet the whole time as they were carefully observing and analyzing what happened.

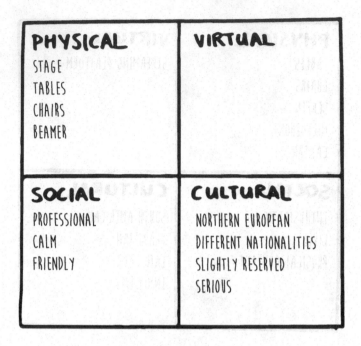

FIGURE 6.10 *The same training in Northern Europe.*

As you can see, the same training in two different environments can be a totally different experience. Especially the social and cultural aspects of these environments made a big difference. Being aware of how an environment affects us is essential for providing learners with a personal, positive, and profound learning experience.

Now go back to your own sheet of paper. When you've completely filled out these four quadrants, you want to figure out how this environment will affect the learner and their experience. If you feel confident that this is the right environment, you're done for now. If you foresee problems with this environment, you need to either solve those problems by altering the environment or choose a different location. For example, if a space is simply too small for the number of learners, you have no choice but to move to a different location. If there are conflicting cultures, such as competitive and collaborative, you might later be able to come up with activities that either solve that problem or even use it to your advantage. For now, you should probably note these conflicting cultures as a constraint.

Later in the design process you might find out that a different environment and/or location is needed. For example, when you test a prototyped experience, you might run into problems with the physical environment. In that case, you need to update these parts on the LX Canvas. This is one example of how the LX Canvas is used dynamically throughout the design process.

Resources

Resources describes everything you have at your disposal for the creation and implementation of your learning experience.

What do you need to create the best learning experience ever? A large sum of money? The fastest laptop? The best creative professionals you can find? No deadlines?

As much as it's fun to dream about the impossible, we must be realistic. In real life we must work with what we've got. That may not sound too promising, but there's good news. Most of the time there are more resources available to you than you might think. I've come up with seven categories: money, time, tools, materials, locations, people, and engagement.

List your resources

Listing resources is relatively easy. Simply look at what is at your disposal in terms of the following categories.

Money

The first resource people tend to think about is money, which makes sense. Having financial resources enables you to buy or rent what you need and hire who you need. The trick is to spend your money wisely since an unlimited budget is highly unlikely.

Time

Time is a valuable resource. Having more time means being able to do more. If you spend your time effectively, the value of time increases. If you waste your time, the value is decreased. Treating time as a resource will help you in designing learning experiences effectively.

Tools

There are many different types of tools you could use to design a learning experience. The design process can benefit from (online) collaboration tools, paper tools like the LX Canvas, or specialist design software.

Materials

I like to use all kinds of materials such as paper, pencils, Play-Doh, yarn, sticky notes, or dice to prototype my designs. It can be inspiring to use these materials and see what happens when your experience comes alive. The key takeaway here is that there are so many materials you can use for LXD if you just give it a try.

Location

As addressed earlier, you need space to learn. This can be a physical space, a virtual space, or a combination of both. Having access to a location can be a huge resource. It's inspiring to see what kind of locations are available to you and to see how these locations can benefit your design.

People

You can do a lot by yourself but not everything. Having the ability to work with other people and use their expertise can dramatically increase the quality of your design. Finding the right people and composing a versatile design team provides a great resource.

Engagement

One of the most powerful resources is people's engagement. If people believe in you, they can help you to find the motivation, inspiration, and ability to make your design a success. Having the engagement of your client, learners, team, and other stakeholders can make all the difference.

Ask for resources

Many resources are easily overlooked, and you want to take some time to look closer at what could be available to you.

So much is possible, and so many people are willing to help or offer resources if they believe in what you are trying to achieve. Just explain what you are working on and ask! You'll be surprised to see the results. Maybe there's a wonderful location offered to you. There might be people who can help you out for a couple of hours.

This is really the story of how LXDCON became a reality. My goal was to bring people together at an event to learn about LXD. Before I knew it, we had a location and a dedicated team of professionals and students to organize the first LXD conference in the world in 2016.

Select your resources

It's critical to consider how you can best use the available resources.

Resources are always a means to an end. You use resources to create an experience that helps the learner reach their goals and achieve the desired learning outcome. Some people let the resources determine what the learning experience will be like.

For example:

"We have to use a tablet to be innovative."

or

"We will use this online game because that's what kids like."

This is the wrong way around. First you decide on the goals you want to achieve, and then you select the resources that will help the learner reach those goals.

Also, don't focus too much on the resources that are easily available to you as they may not be best for your design. For example, you may have a bunch of laptops available, while an educational board game may be a better solution. Just because you've got something doesn't mean you have to use it. And just because you don't have resources doesn't mean you can't find a good alternative. Keep your eyes open to find the resources you need.

Constraints

Constraints include all the limitations to the design, realization, and implementation of a learning experience.

With each learning experience you design, there are limitations to what you can do as a designer. As much as these constraints can sometimes be frustrating, they can also bring out the best in you.

Types of constraints

There are different kinds of constraints you may have to deal with when you design a learning experience. Think about constraints that are:

- Personal
- Practical
- Organizational
- Technological
- Cultural
- Legal

Personal

Nobody's perfect, and we can't do everything we desire. As a professional, it is vital to know both your qualities and your limitations. Don't stretch yourself or your team too far. If you want to use video in a design and you've never shot or edited a video, be careful. Get help when you need it so you don't end up working through the night only to end up with an unfinished product.

Personal limitations also apply to the learner and others who are part of your learning experience. There could be learning disabilities, personal problems, or emotional or mental barriers. Also, think about what you can expect from a teacher, trainer, or subject matter expert.

Practical

Sometimes things are simply impossible for practical reasons: a lack of funds, too little time, no resources, or travel restrictions to name a few. I love to set the bar high for my work and my team. It's easy to get lost in a big idea that sounds great but isn't practical. Who wouldn't want to learn about Roman history in Rome or about marine life scuba diving in the Great Barrier Reef? While that's possible for some, it's out of reach for most of us. If something is practically impossible, don't waste your time on it; find an alternative solution if possible.

Organizational

Through my work as a learning experience designer, trainer, and teacher, I have seen how things work, or don't work, in all kinds of organizations. No two situations are the same, and sometimes the work I can do with and for a client, trainee, or student is rather limited. More often though, a lot is possible, and the constraints can be worked through.

Understanding the organizational needs, rules, regulations, possibilities, and limitations is essential to working effectively and getting the most out of the situation.

Technological

Technology is great and allows us to do amazing things, if it works! It happens to the best of us. You've tested and checked everything and for no obvious reasons a computer crashes and leaves you scrambling for a solution. Incidental things can and will happen from time to time, and having a backup plan is essential.

There are also given technological limitations, like when I worked on a collaborative design for students in Europe and Africa. The African students lived in a rural area where internet access was limited to an old dial-in modem. The solution was to make a super simple and effective website that allowed for online and offline work which limited data transfer enormously.

Cultural

When you use humor in your design, there is a chance that some people will laugh, others won't, and some feel offended. My team once used a depiction of Christ in a cartoony way, which was not appreciated. What seemed harmless to us was harmful to others. Cultural differences might be limiting, but they are important to consider.

Cultural diversity is enriching and inspiring. Knowing what you can and can't do in a country, region, school, or company is essential for a successful design.

Legal

This might be last on this list, but it is definitely not the least important constraint. I probably don't have to explain that you don't want to break the law. Depending on the county you're in and the organization you are designing for, there will be different laws, rules, and regulations to keep in mind. Some things to look at are dealing with intellectual property, sensitive content, contractual obligations, or liability.

I've designed learning experiences that were mandatory for employees who are required to have a certain level of expertise by law. You can come up with amazing designs, but you can't leave out essential information, and you need to make sure the results are there.

How to list and deal with constraints

The idea is to consider the main limitations that affect this learning experience and plan how to work around them.

Listing the constraints is a matter of looking carefully at all personal, practical, organizational, technological, cultural, and legal constraints. Figure out what applies to your design and make sure to dig deeper if in doubt, especially in regard to laws, rules, and regulations. When your list is complete, think about how these constraints affect the learning experience. If you feel there are serious limitations, try to find a way to work around them.

Constraints may limit your options, but they should never limit your creativity. In fact, they should enhance your creativity. Finding creative solutions to deal with these limitations will only make your design better.

There's a fun thought experiment you can do to deal with constraints. Let's say that a small budget is a major constraint. Now imagine there is no budget at all, and you still want to design the best possible learning experience. You might come up with a cheap idea that works wonderfully well. Or you might find sponsors for your design because you have a convincing case of how a bit more money would make a big difference for the learner. Either way, doing less with more requires creativity and determination, and you can never get enough of that.

Strategy

A strategy is a set of design guidelines based on the work you've done so far in your exploration.

Look carefully at the results from the first eight steps of the LX Canvas: learning outcome, learning objectives, people, characteristics, location, environment, resources, and constraints.

Writing a strategy is one of the hardest parts of using the LX Canvas. The reason for this is that you are switching between a more analytical mindset to a more creative mindset. A good strategy builds a bridge between the exploration and the creation of your learning experience.

It's all about making connections between the different elements on the LX Canvas. These connections offer valuable insights into the dos and don'ts of your design. A connection is made between two or more elements. For example, you can look at a specific learning objective and your resources. If there is a resource that is perfect for reaching that goal, it would be a strategic decision to make use of that.

Having a good strategy before you start ideation will help guide your design process, focus your creativity, and ensure that what you design is aligned with the goals and needs of the learner. First you strategize; then you come up with your ideas and designs.

How to write a strategy

There are several ways to write a strategy. Generally, I prefer to use the "if … then …" construction. This is a simple and effective way to get started.

I just talked about using a specific resource to reach a learning objective. Let's say that the learning objective is effective online communication and the resource is the phone of the learner. That would look like this:

> *If* we want our learners to be able to communicate more effectively online, *then* they could use their own phones.

This would be an even better strategic choice if you could add more elements and an explanation. Imagine a major constraint is lack of budget.

If we want our learners to be able to communicate more effectively online, then they could use their own phones, especially since we have a very limited budget.

This is a rather obvious strategic choice. Some will be less obvious and harder to spot. That's when it becomes a bit of a puzzle and you might need to dig a bit deeper.

Start by combining just two elements and try to add more as you proceed. I do enjoy uncovering less obvious connections and coming up with a clever strategy. It's a fun challenge that can really pay off.

Here are some examples of strategies:

> If time is limited (constraint), then we should focus on the most important goals (learning objectives) and not worry about goals that are nice to have (learning objectives).

> If some of the learners (people) are afraid of change (characteristic), then we need to address these emotions early on (process) to ensure they can grow as a group (learning outcome).

> If university students (people) must learn to solve complex problems (learning objectives), then we need to work in multidisciplinary groups (activities) to ensure various perspectives are being included (learning objective) in problem solving.

> If the needs of the client (learning outcome) can contradict some goals of the learner (learning objectives), then we could invite the client to participate.

Categorize your strategy

Once you've formulated various strategic guidelines, it might be helpful to categorize them. Having a categorized strategic list offers a better overview and makes it easier to use than a long list of different items. What categories you choose depends on the learning experience you design. Generally, it's a good idea to base categories on the learner and the learning outcome/objectives.

What is not a strategy

You've just seen examples of well-formulated strategies. The biggest pitfall in writing a strategy is to start designing instead of strategizing. I see this happen all the time, and I'd like to illustrate this with some examples.

- Play a game

- Do an online treasure quest

- Use video

- Implement microlearning

- Make it fun

What's wrong with this? Playing a game, doing an online treasure quest, or watching a video are *activities* and not strategies. During the strategy phase, you are not designing but strategizing; that's a big difference. You need to formulate a strategy that enables you to design activities and not simply state what the activity is going to be.

With the last two examples, it's not clear why you are choosing this strategy. Why would you use microlearning? Why it is a strategic choice? If you found out through design research that the learner would prefer loads of short activities and it serves their goals, then document that reasoning. Using the "if...then..." construction, you could say:

> "If we know that our learners would prefer playing more short activities over fewer longer ones, we could use microlearning for this experience."

Always explain why a strategic choice is made and
base it on what you see on the LX Canvas.

A strategy like "make it fun" is just too general and a bit nonsensical. What would be the alternative? Make it boring? Use terms that you can work with like *playful* or *entertaining*. When you use those terms, always explain why the experience should be that way. Here's an example:

"If the learners aren't very motivated (characteristic) to participate, we could make the start of the experience (process) entertaining to get them excited and ready to learn."

In this example, you can see the direction your design is headed without determining what the design is going to be. Starting with an entertaining activity can be done in many ways.

Here's a challenge for you: How many kinds of entertaining activities can you come up with in one minute? Time starts now! This short challenge illustrates the difference between having an idea and having a strategy.

Postponing ideation

Taking the time to write a strategy accomplishes two very important things:

- It helps you to design more effectively.

- It postpones ideation.

When we are part of a creative process, ideas can pop into our minds all the time. Often, this starts at the very beginning of a project.

Imagine, while kicking off a project, a client saying she would like her employees to collaborate more effectively. Your first response could be:

"I know about this collaborative game that we could tweak and make it work for your employees."

Whether this idea would work or not doesn't really matter. What you've just done is sabotage the creative process. Either you go with this idea, therefore completely skipping further research and ideation, or your idea will linger in the back of your mind while limiting coming up with fresh ideas.

Ideation is not a matter of listing existing ideas; it is about generating new and original ideas that work. The strategy forces you to think about the direction your creative process is going based on what you've learned from your design research and analysis. Once you have your strategy, it guides you toward the ideas and designs that work best for your learners and their goals.

Activities

Now we are into the design phase!
Activities are what the learner actually does to learn.

What is the learner going to do in the learning experience you design? Answering that question is a vital part of your job as a learning experience designer. When you design a learning experience, you are finding ways to activate the learner.

Traditionally, we might focus on what the teacher or trainer does to enable the student or trainee to learn. For example, schoolbooks are structured in a practical way that enables the teacher to teach, such as by dividing the topic into smaller parts that fit the duration of a class.

In LXD we focus on what the learner is going to do and how they learn from what they experience. Others might be there to support them, but the activities of the learner are always leading.

Begin with strategy

The logical way to get started is to select one or more learning objectives from your LX Canvas to work with. Preferably you would select primary learning objectives as they are vital to the overall learning experience.

Once you have selected your learning objectives, take a good look at your strategy. What are the things that you need to keep in mind as you design this activity? There could be an obvious direction for your design based on your strategy. The characteristics of the learner could call for a certain type of activity, especially when you combine it with a suitable location.

For example, if you design an activity for hyperactive 6-year-olds and you have a gym facility at your disposal, you want to use that to your advantage. It would be the perfect place to utilize their energy in a fun and active experience.

Ideation

With your strategy in mind, it's time to generate ideas for your design. This can relate to individual activities or to the overall learning experience. For example, when I worked on a game on safety in schools, I focused on generating game ideas first. I didn't worry too much about the rest of the experience yet. The game is such a vital part of the experience that it pays off to focus your attention on that first.

If you don't have one specific activity that stands out, you want to come up with more general ideas for the overall learning experience. From there you can generate ideas for activities that fit into the bigger picture.

Don't lock into one or two ideas straightaway. Enjoy your creative freedom to come up with a variety of ideas in different directions before you select the most promising ones.

As described earlier, to turn your idea into a learning experience, you need to conceptualize, visualize, and prototype your design. While these steps are always the same, the process is never identical. Some designs are relatively easy; others take a lot of effort and iterations. If needed, take a moment to refer to Chapter 5, "How to design a learning experience."

Before you finish designing activities, ask yourself these questions:

- Is the activity I designed in line with my strategy?

- Will this activity enable the learner to achieve the learning objectives that I selected?

- Will all activities combined enable the learner to achieve the desired learning outcome?

- Are these activities positive, personal, and profound?

If one or more of the answers to this question is no, then you're not done with your design. Use these questions as a checklist. It's easy to forget about the strategy when you're having fun brainstorming. Maybe one or two learning objectives are not covered in your design, which can undermine achieving the desired learning outcome. Have fun with the design process, and be sure to check if your amazing, crazy, original, and innovative ideas get the job done! There's only one section left of the LX Canvas, the second part of the design phase.

Process

Process describes the actual learning experience as it takes place over time. It is an arranged and scheduled set of activities.

It's about time we talked about time.

Time is inseparable from experience. Just like listening to a piece of music, an experience takes place over time, and without time, there is no experience. The process you design is based on time and how it is spent.

Every moment that passes in time is impossible to get back. Once it is gone, it is gone forever. Your goal is to design a learning experience that is of real value to the learner. It needs to be valuable enough to make it worth spending their own time by giving them something in return for the time they will never get back. And that is quite a challenge.

So, before you finalize the design of your learning experience, ask yourself this question:

"Is the time that I'm asking of the learner invested wisely?"

Maybe you could save time cutting an activity a bit short. Or maybe you could make an activity (even) more appealing and engaging. Whatever you do, don't waste any time; it just too precious.

Let's assume you have designed several activities for your learning experience. Now you are going to take these activities and place them in a process that should lead to achieving the desired learning outcome. To do that, you need to answer a few questions.

When will the learning experience take place?

The primary purpose of designing a process is to decide what happens when. First, you should determine when the learning experience starts and when it ends. Keep in mind that the end of a learning experience doesn't mean you stop learning. There are numerous ways to extend the learning experience. For example, you might offer tools or other resources that the learners can apply and use long after the learning experience has officially ended. Think about how the learner will exit the experience and how it will continue to impact their lives.

When will activities take place?

The word *when* encompasses in what order, for how long, and at what time the activities you've designed will take place (see **FIGURE 6.11**).

When my team and I were organizing our first LXD conference in 2016, we spent a lot of time figuring out the program. A program is not just a list of activities; it is the structure behind the experience of the participant. We had some wild ideas and timing was everything. You want to balance more passive activities such as talks with more interactive activities such as design workshops. Also, you want to give people enough time to process everything, kick back for a moment with a cup of coffee, and enjoy a spontaneous conversation. From start to end, it all has to fit within the timeframe in a way that works well for all participants.

To get started on the process, you need an indication of the duration of the overall experience. A learning experience can include multiple activities. You must decide on the right order for these activities to take place. Some choices can be easy like putting reflection after and not before the activity you want to reflect on. In other cases, it can be more complex, especially with custom-designed activities. Sometimes you may need to test different orders of activities to learn what works best.

Also, you want to think about how long each activity takes. Knowing that the attention span of learners is generally limited, you can imagine that you want to keep things short or at least not longer than necessary.

FIGURE 6.11 *First LXD conference in 2016. (Photo courtesy of Alex in 't Veld.)*

Now that you know in what order and for how long activities will take place, you want to figure out when each activity takes place. This is an important step because it determines the pace and flow of your learning experience.

A good pace gives the learner time to digest each activity. Sometimes we need some time to let things sink in and including this time in your design really makes a difference. A 30-minute break or a night's sleep can fundamentally change the quality of a learning experience. That's why you design both for the time activities take place and for the time between each activity.

What is the learner journey?

What will the complete learning experience look like for the learner?

Once you have worked out what happens when in terms of the activities and the overall structure, you can add more levels of detail. A great way to do that is by visualizing the learner journey. This is a step-by-step path that offers insight into the overall experience of the learner. An important part of any learner journey is the emotion of the learner. How you feel influences how you learn. As stated in one of the rules of LXD in this book, learning is influenced by emotion.

The importance of emotions in learning cannot be understated. Having an emotional map as part of the learner journey can help improve your design and the overall quality of the learning experience. When you know how learners generally feel at different points in time, you can deal with those emotions respectfully and effectively.

Experience mapping is a field on its own, and in the next chapter it will be discussed together with other design tools and methodologies.

Using the LX Canvas

You've gotten to know all elements on the LX Canvas. Now it's time to put it into practice. There are different ways you can use the LX Canvas effectively. Let's explore them.

Every time you use the LX Canvas, you will learn new things. That's what I've experienced during countless design sessions. On the surface, the LX Canvas is relatively easy to understand. If you know the elements, you can start using it. Once you dig deeper, you will find multiple layers of depth to using the LX Canvas as you develop and refine your analytical and creative skills.

Ways to use the LX Canvas

You can use the LX Canvas in all kinds of situations.

- Create a quick overview for yourself and your client to gain a better understanding of the purpose and context of your design.

- Co-create the designs of activities with learners, experts, clients, and/or other stakeholders. Use the LX Canvas to structure these sessions.

- Have a design session with your design team. This can range from 30 minutes to one or more days, depending on what's needed.

- Analyze an existing learning experience when creating a redesign. This helps to spot areas that need be improved and to discover strengths of the experience.

- Write down the findings from your design research and see if there's something missing. If there are no gaps, you are ready to start working on your design.

- When you're working with a large group of people, divide them into small teams and let each team complete their own LX Canvas. Compare the results at the end.

Choose your approach

When you work with the LX Canvas, you can use the approach that works best for you. Remember that there is a "how to" written for each element of the LX Canvas in this chapter.

The easiest way to start working with the LX Canvas is by doing it step-by-step. Simply use the order from this book. Start with the learning outcome and finish with the process.

Once you've completed all 11 elements, you have a great overview, and it's easier to see which elements still need some work. For example, you might need to know a bit more about the location you selected or one of the activities doesn't fit the process.

Try to complete the LX Canvas relatively quickly for a first-draft design. Just because you started working step-by-step doesn't mean you can't go back. Nothing is set in stone; you can always change things.

You can start by looking at the things that you already know and add them to the LX Canvas straightaway. For example, you have a learning outcome, a list of people, a location, and some resources. This would leave several parts of the LX Canvas open or incomplete, but that's OK for now. Having just a partial overview is already helpful as you understand what you're dealing with. As you continue, you know what's missing and where to focus your design research. This makes the process much more effective.

Finally, you can also use the LX Canvas in a dynamic and iterative way. That's my personal preference as it allows me to try, test, and learn things as I go along.

Back when I taught LXD at Avans University of Applied Sciences in the Netherlands, I learned a lot from how my students used the LX Canvas. They thought of it as foundational to their design process. With each new idea, design, or prototype, they would go back to the LX Canvas and see if everything was still aligned with their strategy and findings. If not, they would reconsider their options. They would frequently do a bit more research or testing and update their findings on the LX Canvas.

The results were impressive. When you compare their work with earlier students who did not have access to the LX Canvas, the difference was significant. In previous years, students struggled more, and there tended to be some clear weak spots in their designs. Working with the LX Canvas made the weak spots mostly disappear and improved the overall quality of their designs. Seeing these improvements strengthened my belief in the LX Canvas and the power of LXD.

◾ Enjoy the LX Canvas

We've stepped through the exploration phase, looking closely at personal and situation factors and determining strategy. Then we've had fun coming up with the strategy and activities, jumping back into exploration as needed.

Like a painting, the LX Canvas is never really finished. It is a dynamic document that evolves as you proceed. With each iteration you gain new insights as you get closer to your final design. Use it as a creative tool to boost your design process and to create incredible learning experiences. Combine the LX Canvas with the tools in the next chapter to do your best work. Enjoy!

*If people knew how hard I worked
to get my mastery, it wouldn't
seem so wonderful at all.*

—MICHELANGELO, ARTIST

Chapter 7

Design tools

I ♡ TO USE

Having the right tools can make a big difference. You've already gotten to know the Learning Experience Canvas (LX Canvas), and now you will get to know three more design tools.

Give a carpenter a saw, a hammer, and some nails and you can expect great things. Give me the same tools and you won't get anything solid, usable, or practical. Who uses a tool is more important than the quality of the tool itself. While I believe the tools that I'm about to discuss are powerful and valuable, it's up to you to get the most out of them. Good luck!

Specifically, we'll look in detail at personas, empathy maps, and experience maps.

Personas

A great way to get a clear picture of the people you design for is by creating a persona. This is a fictional archetypical character that represents a larger group of people.

Personas come from the field of interaction design where they help to understand the needs, experiences, behaviors, and goals of users. While a user and a learner are fundamentally different, the principles used to create and apply personas work just as well in learning experience design (LXD).

According to designer Alan Cooper, "Personas are the single most powerful design tool that we use. They are the foundation for all subsequent goal-directed design. Personas allow us to see the scope and nature of the design problem. [They] are the bright light under which we do surgery."

Personas should always be based on design research. In other words, you must understand who your learner is and be able to empathize with them. Once you've done your research and you've gotten to know the learner, you can start working on a persona.

Try to make the persona as realistic as possible with a photo, name, age, profession, cultural background, personal interests, and hobbies. Using this data, you can write a short story that makes your persona come alive. Of course, you want to relate the persona and their story to the learning experience you design. How does the topic and/or outcome of your learning experience play a role in the life of the persona? Having general information with no relation to the purpose of your design will tend to lead to a generic design.

For example, what if you design a learning experience for French students who struggle in school? A boy, 8 years old, who lives in Marseille and likes Pokémon is too general. Instead, try to make it more specific and relevant:

> Eight-year-old Bilal from Marseille is a bright student, but he is performing poorly in school because he's being bullied. On his way to school, and during breaks, a group of classmates harasses him. Yesterday, they stole some of his beloved Pokémon cards. His parents are worried about his performance, but he's ashamed to tell them about being bullied.

When you read Bilal's story, you empathize with him, and you can start generating ideas on how to support him through your design. Things like the bullying, him being ashamed, and his parents being worried are all clear indicators of the problems you need to solve and how to solve them.

Bilal represents a group of students who can do much better but for some reason don't. For this design you probably need more personas to have a broader representation of this struggling group. The reasons they struggle, the things they (like to) do, and the ways you are able to serve them, can be very different from their peers. Students can perform poorly because of poverty and not getting three meals per day. Or they may struggle because of exam stress.

If you figure out why they do the things they do, you can find solutions that work for them. Identifying different groups based on their behavior works much better than creating groups based only on demographics. You focus on what learners do in daily life and create a design that fits into their world and serves them best.

The benefits of working with personas

There are few things that I love about working with personas.

A well-crafted persona communicates clearly who your design is for. It represents the data from your design research in a personal way that is easy to understand.

Personas can help you throughout the design process. As silly as it sounds, I like to talk to the persona.

Let's say your persona is a 35-year-old female scientist from Montreal, Canada, named Maria Dupont. With every design decision you make you can ask:

"Would this work for Maria?"

or

"Would Maria prefer option A over option B?"

Having a persona makes it easier to make choices during the design process.

It can also prevent the so-called flexible user. Without a persona, you can easily forget what matters most to the learner. Before you know it, you start adding things that you think the learner will use and appreciate, even though they add no actual value. Going back to your persona will prevent learning experiences that are bloated and irrelevant.

How to create a persona

Start by defining the basic demographics of your persona. Of course, all names chosen should be made-up names, which is true of all examples in this book.

Be careful not to create an image that is stereotypical, discriminating, and/or racist. Don't give into assumptions, prejudice, or bias, and use data gathered from your design research to paint a realistic, unbiased, and fair image.

- **Age.** How old is your persona? Looking at the average age of your learners is a great indicator for choosing an age. Of course, if you have two distinctly different age groups, like parents and children, you don't want to use the average age. This would require two different personas to adequately represent both groups of learners.

- **Gender.** Next, look at the female/male/other ratio to decide on the sex of your persona. Sometimes it's obvious, and the choice is easy to make. If there is no clear majority, you can either pick one or decide to create multiple personas to ensure all groups are represented. This principle applies to all aspects of your persona. Try to limit the number of personas as much as you can without missing out on any major distinct groups.

- **Location.** Where is your persona from? Pick a country and a city within that country for your persona. For larger cities, a specific neighborhood or area is a good idea.

- **Name.** Give your persona a name. This is a fun part that is easily underestimated. Picking a name is harder than it might sound. A name represents more than a person.

Let's pause and consider how a name can represent a nationality, ethnicity, and culture. Just compare Günther Hoffman to Darren Thompson or Mohammed Bakir. You probably think you can tell who lives in Australia, Morocco, or Germany. What if I told you that Mohammed is the one who lives in Germany, Darren is an expat living in Morocco, and Günther is enjoying retirement on the Gold Coast of Australia? That changes the whole narrative.

You must be careful with clichés and be aware of the implications of the name you choose. It should be representative in a sensible, realistic, and respectful way. A good idea is to combine slight adaptations of first and last names from different learners you have researched.

- **Occupation.** Time to add an occupation to your learner. When you are designing a learning experience for managers at a specific company, the choice is made for you. Or when your learner is a K–12 student, that's easy. If your design is for different types of learners, you must make a choice. Try to see what type of occupations are common and pick one that makes the most sense.

- **Education.** Since we are designing for learners, their level of education is an important fact. Their education isn't just an indicator of their cognitive abilities or intelligence. It also says something about their needs, preferences, and expectations. A learner with a PhD will probably appreciate a different type of experience than a high school dropout. As a designer, I don't have a preference for any type of learner; I just want to offer them the best possible experience.

- **Family.** What is the family situation of your learner? Is it a schoolgirl living with her single mother and younger brother? Or a married man with no kids? Family is a big part of our lives; it says a lot about where we come from and what our daily life looks like.

- **Picture.** Right about now you can add a picture of your learner. This can be an illustration or a photo. It is another fun part of creating a persona. A picture tells a thousand words, so choose wisely. Always be careful with using personal photos and/or copyrighted material.

The demographics are the foundation of your persona. Now you are going to breathe life into it.

- **Bio.** Make your persona come alive by adding a short story about the daily life of the learner. How do they spend their time, what are the things they like to do, what are the struggles they experience? There is no recipe for this part; it's up to you to write a believable bio. Make sure that you include aspects of their lives that relate to the topic of your learning experience. For example, I wrote stories for students in a special needs school for whom we would design a digital learning platform. In their stories I included some of the struggles these students have in school as well as the things that they enjoy and are good at both inside and outside school. This creates a balanced and realistic image of who these students are and offers strategic insights for the design process.

With the demographics and story done, it's time to add a one or two more elements. Which elements you add is up to you and depends on the type of design you are creating. **FIGURE 7.1** shows some suggestions. Pick what works for you, and you've completed your persona.

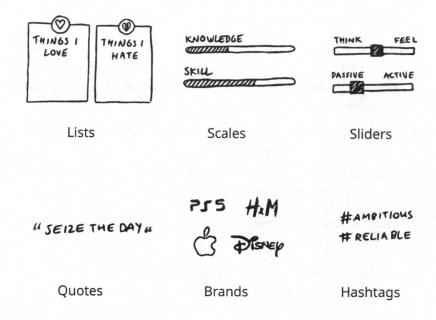

FIGURE 7.1 *Add a distinctive element to your personas that make sense for your project — here are six ideas.*

Before you finalize your persona, it's a good idea to show it to some of the people who this persona represents. If they recognize themselves and deem it believable, you're done. If they don't, you want to use their feedback to improve your persona. Testing your persona ensures you are on the right track, especially when it comes to sensitive topics such as age, gender, nationality, and culture.

Example personas

Much of my work revolves around supporting learning experience designers from around the world. To do that successfully I need to know who they are, where they are from, and what they are looking for.

My team and I developed three personas to represent the global LXD community (**FIGURES 7.2**, **7.3**, and **7.4**). Each persona has their own needs and goals in relation to LXD. Having these personas has helped us greatly with designing our courses, producing the website LXD.org, and organizing our LXDCON events. All three personas are based on data we gathered over the years from web analytics, feedback from trainees, questionnaires filled out by attendees of our events, and other interactions like chats or interviews we've had with community members around the globe. These rich resources of qualitative and quantitative data allowed us to create realistic personas.

Our three personas are primarily based on their level of expertise in LXD. We have novice, intermediate, and advanced personas. Together they represent the whole LXD community in a realistic way. Individually they represent specific needs of parts of the LXD community.

We used these personas to determine what kind of services we offer as an LXD training agency, LXD event organizer, and driving force in the LXD community. This has been handy to structure LXD.org based on different use cases.

For example, the novice persona represents the largest group of community members, and they are primarily looking for a definition of LXD, basic LXD knowledge, and the Learning Experience Canvas. We've made these elements easily accessible, which worked out perfectly. When you look at the highest-ranked pages, these are exactly the things that are most accessed.

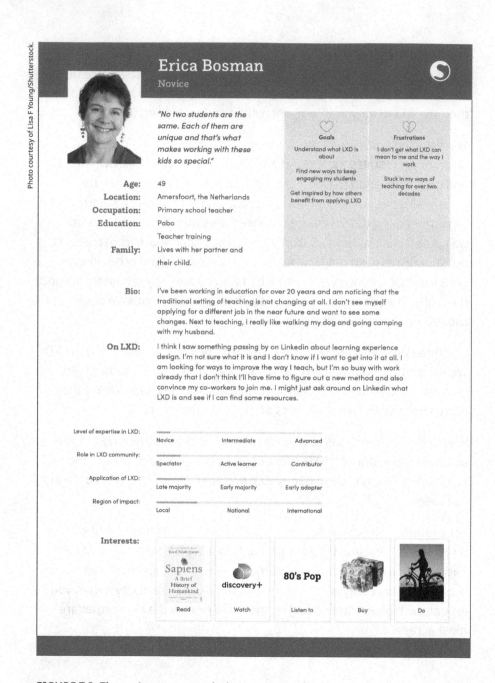

Erica Bosman
Novice

"No two students are the same. Each of them are unique and that's what makes working with these kids so special."

Goals
Understand what LXD is about

Find new ways to keep engaging my students

Get inspired by how others benefit from applying LXD

Frustrations
I don't get what LXD can mean to me and the way I work

Stuck in my ways of teaching for over two decades

Age: 49
Location: Amersfoort, the Netherlands
Occupation: Primary school teacher
Education: Pabo
Teacher training
Family: Lives with her partner and their child.

Bio: I've been working in education for over 20 years and am noticing that the traditional setting of teaching is not changing at all. I don't see myself applying for a different job in the near future and want to see some changes. Next to teaching, I really like walking my dog and going camping with my husband.

On LXD: I think I saw something passing by on Linkedin about learning experience design. I'm not sure what it is and I don't know if I want to get into it at all. I am looking for ways to improve the way I teach, but I'm so busy with work already that I don't think I'll have time to figure out a new method and also convince my co-workers to join me. I might just ask around on Linkedin what LXD is and see if I can find some resources.

Level of expertise in LXD:
Novice   Intermediate   Advanced

Role in LXD community:
Spectator   Active learner   Contributor

Application of LXD:
Late majority   Early majority   Early adopter

Region of impact:
Local   National   International

Interests:

Sapiens A Brief History of Humankind	discovery+	80's Pop		
Read	Watch	Listen to	Buy	Do

FIGURE 7.2 *The novice represents the largest group of learners.*

Kevin Chang
Intermediate

"Seize the day."

Goals
Apply LXD in my current design process to facilitate myself and my clients

Keep users or learners centered in my designs

Frustrations
I don't know where to start as I do know UX but not LX

Looking for practices or a training to get more insight into applying LXD

Age: 28
Location: Singapore, Singapore
Occupation: User experience designer
Education: University of Queensland
Multimedia design
Family: Single

Bio: After studying Multimedia design in Australia, I came back home and started a small web design company with some friends that I knew from university. Now I feel like I should be more versatile than just a UX designer and really want to focus on experiences. Next to designing, I also really like to practice photography.

On LXD: As a designer, I'm always interested in other design disciplines. LXD was something I came across after reading a blog about the difference between LXD and instructional design. I got curious and downloaded the LX Canvas to try it out, but I can't really decide when to adopt LXD in my current design process.

Level of expertise in LXD:
Novice   Intermediate   Advanced

Role in LXD community:
Spectator   Active learner   Contributor

Application of LXD:
Late majority   Early majority   Early adopter

Region of impact:
Local   National   International

Interests:

WIRED	NETFLIX	Dance		
Read	Watch	Listen to	Buy	Do

FIGURE 7.3 *The intermediate learner is often active in the experience.*

Jessica Culbert
Advanced

"I'm just curious by nature, always trying new things and figuring out how stuff works."

Goals
- Lifelong learning
- Making a difference in people's lives
- Contribute to the development of LXD
- Play an active part in the global LXD community

Frustrations
- Lack of understanding and support from colleagues
- The slow acceptance of new ideas and technologies in learning

Age: 41

Location: San Francisco, USA

Occupation: Learning experience designer

Education: University of Washington
Learning sciences

Family: Lives with her partner and two children.

Bio: I'm currently working at an international company at the HR department as project lead. We do both e-learning and blended learning projects with a team of designers and developers. When I'm not working I enjoy family time, read a lot of books (fiction and nonfiction) and I try to stay active by running.

On LXD: About three years ago I discovered learning experience design and it made total sense to me. I've always enjoyed combining my scientific background with a more creative approach. My colleagues tend to have different views as they are less open to change. That's why I loved to meet like-minded people at a learning experience design conference. It's good to know that I'm not the only one out there. What I'd like to see, is more scientific evidence on how (good) learning experience design works.

Level of expertise in LXD:

Novice	Intermediate	Advanced

Role in LXD community:

Spectator	Active learner	Contributor

Application of LXD:

Late majority	Early majority	Early adopter

Region of impact:

Local	National	International

Interests:

LXD BLOG	Disney+	Pop		
Read	Watch	Listen to	Buy	Do

FIGURE 7.4 *The needs of the advanced learner are significantly different.*

Empathy map

Empathy is a vital skill for learning experience designers.
It allows you to see the world through the eyes of the learner.

Creating an empathy map for your learners can enhance your ability to empathize and improve the quality of your designs.

The ability to empathize is not a talent; it's a skill. Empathy is a skill you can develop through practice. Every time I research learners, I improve my ability to empathize. Gaining a deep understanding of the people — the people you design for is more than a necessity; it's part of what makes my work so endlessly interesting and enjoyable. People in all their diversity and uniqueness are the heart of your design and your design process.

Empathy mapping as a method

The original empathy map was created by Dave Gray as part of a human-centered design toolkit. The purpose of an empathy map is to develop a deep, shared understanding and empathy for the people you design for. Over the years the empathy map has evolved, and several adaptations have been made to serve specific purposes, for example to empathize with the user of an app, the customer of a supermarket, or a patient in a hospital.

As much as I love the original empathy map, it is not ideal for learners. That's why I created a different empathy map specifically for learners (**FIGURE 7.5**).

If you're already familiar with the original empathy map, it's easy to spot the similarities. When you look a bit closer, there are several obvious differences that make this empathy map more suitable for learners. First, the four main quadrants are divided into two triangular parts. Each triangle has a question to answer about the learner. When you answer all eight questions, you'll end up with a detailed view of who the learner is and how they feel.

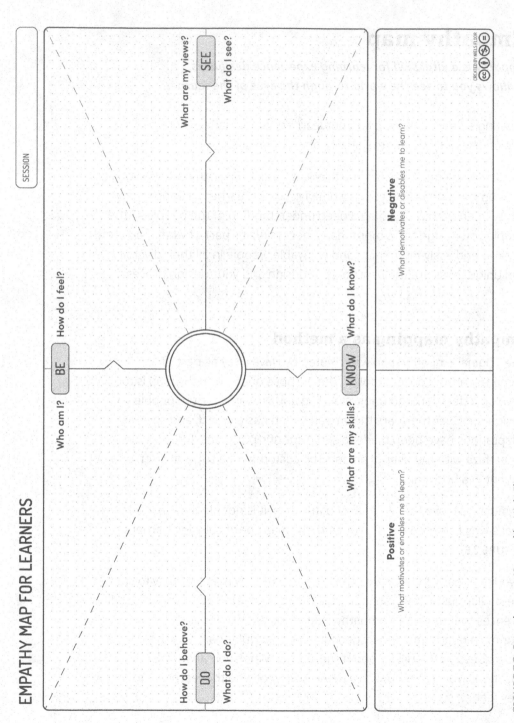

FIGURE 7.5 *Empathy map. (Created by Niels Floor)*

How to map empathy

It's obvious that you need to interact with the learner you're mapping, so let's assume you're talking to the learner right now. Also, you need to have a clear idea of the learning outcome that the learner would like and/or need to achieve.

Example:

The learner wants to learn how to deliver a great presentation for a large audience. The outcome would be about feeling confident, inspiring other people, and being successful.

Write down the date and name of the session in the top-right corner.

Example:

15 September 2022 presentation project.

Start by asking the question "Who am I?" ("Who are you?") This is a relatively simple question with a factual answer.

Example:

Jennifer Duncan, 35 years old, Boston, USA, account manager at Cisco, mother of three children.

Now answer the rest of the questions in clockwise order. It's important to relate every question to the desired learning outcome.

Example for "How do I feel?" question:

How do you feel about delivering presentations? The answer could be: "It stresses me out because I don't feel confident talking in front of large groups."

After answering these questions, formulate the positive and negative aspects that would motivate or enable the learner to be successful and vice versa. Most answers can be found in the previously answered questions. Others could arise from specifically asking about the positives and negatives to the learner.

Example:

Negative: Fear of public speaking (based on the "How do I feel?" question).

Positive: I'd like to be more confident in general.

Finally, add a picture of the learner in the center of the empathy map. This completes the empathy map and makes it much easier to remember the learner and empathize with them.

Important to know

Following these steps should get you on the right track. There are a couple of things that are vital to keep in mind, though.

An empathy map is just a tool; how you use it determines the quality of the insights you gain and the extent to which you're able to empathize. It takes time and effort to use them.

You can create empathy maps in different phases of the design process, not just at the start as part of your research. For example, you can also use it to let the learner reflect on the actual learning experience.

People change and so will your empathy map. The answers on the empathy map depend on the moment you use it. Don't be afraid to update an empathy map occasionally.

Empathy map examples

I've used empathy maps when developing the e-learning course on color theory we did for AkzoNobel, a leading paint and coatings company. Akzo-Nobel is active in more than 150 countries, which means its employees are from all over the world. We wanted to gain a better understanding of the learner and research cultural differences and similarities.

For example, in some countries, companies operate in a more hierarchical way than in others. This influences the learning experience. One employee is told by their boss to do the e-learning, while another chooses to do so. Or some will be expected to complete the e-learning in their spare time, while others can finish it during office hours. Being at home in the evening or in the office during the day is also a big difference.

The examples of the empathy maps for AkzoNobel show two fictional characters who represent larger groups of employees in different parts of the world. We used empathy mapping in a similar way as creating a persona.

These empathy maps are based on design research and enable us to map out who our learners are and what they expect from participating in a e-learning module on color theory. Our goal was to create an e-learning that is nontraditional and offers a surprising, challenging, and enlightening experience. The question is, what are the expectations of the learners, and how will they react to something they are not used to?

The empathy map in **FIGURE 7.6** tells the story of Clarissa from São Paulo, Brazil. She is obligated to do the e-learning and not particularly looking forward to it. Color theory may sound a bit boring to her as she prefers to keep it practical and applicable. At the same time, she enjoys her work and loves color. The e-learning module is different from what she expects, and as she proceeds, she starts to enjoy it.

The empathy map of Daniel from London, UK shows a young, ambitious employee (**FIGURE 7.7**). He chooses to participate in the e-learning course and is determined to get a high score. Even though he knows very little about color, he is eager to learn. Daniel loves a challenge but doesn't want to waste time. As soon as he starts, he is surprised because this is not what he expects from an e-learning course. It is a positive surprise, though. He loves that there is optional information to go more in depth.

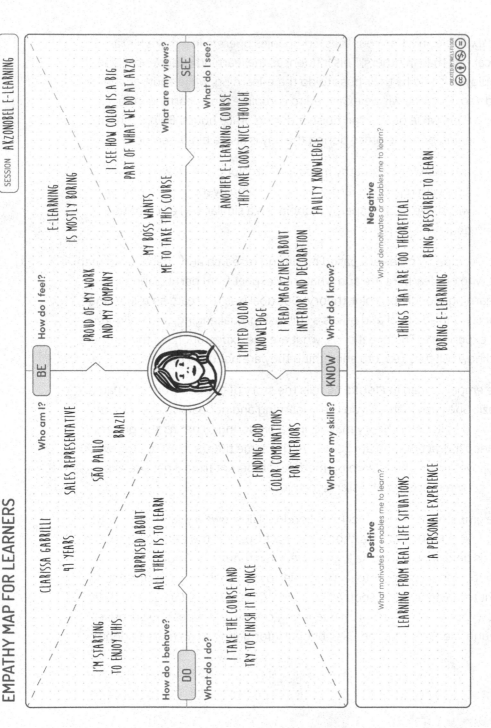

FIGURE 7.6 *Empathy map for Clarissa who finds e-learning boring.*

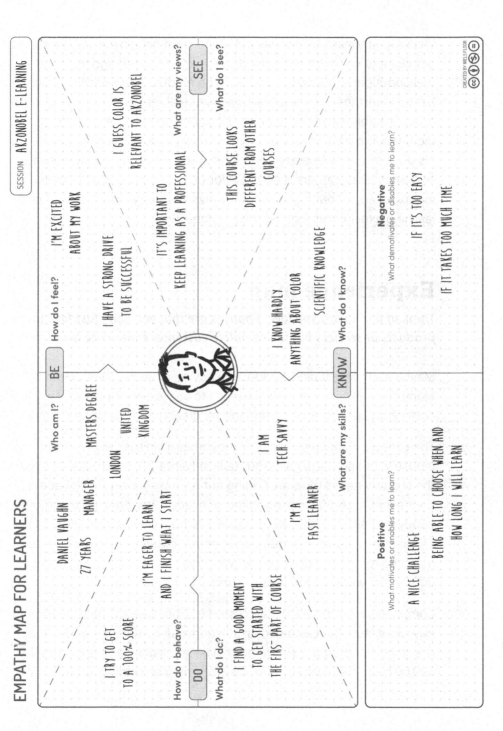

FIGURE 7.7 *Empathy map for Daniel who loves a challenge.*

The empathy maps of Clarissa and Daniel have helped me, my team, and our client to gain a better understanding of who we design for, how they feel about participating in our e-learning module, and what we can do to best support them. For example, we used real-life situations to make the topic relatable with Clarissa in mind. For Daniel there are opportunities to dig deeper into the theory of color, which satisfies his learning needs and his drive to complete every part of the module. Knowing what motivates or demotivates learners is essential for providing them with a great learning experience. Creating an empathy map enables you to design personal learning experiences that get the job done.

Experience map

Think of a company you love. Chances are that you don't just love their products or services but the complete customer experience they offer.

Maybe it's their fast delivery, valuable advice, or an excellent help desk. Many companies use experience maps to analyze and optimize their customer experiences. Wouldn't this be great for education as well?

The concept of mapping experiences comes from the service design industry. The goal is to gain a strategic advantage by understanding what the customer goes through, finding out what they love (or hate) about their experience, and improve things if needed. It keeps the customers happy and the company successful. Any school would be interested in offering their students a great experience. So why not use experience mapping to help you achieve this? Well, you can. But there are a couple of differences you'll want to keep in mind.

Companies want to satisfy their customers, because satisfied customers buy more stuff. But customer satisfaction and learner satisfaction are not the same. For example, you want to make everything as easy as possible for the customer. Learning isn't easy. Learning something new takes you out of your comfort zone. In fact, you need to be challenged to really progress. Imagine making ordering a pair of shoes a challenge; good luck selling them.

There's a difference between buying a TV and learning physics. The process of learning is often more complex, not only because learning takes longer but also because there are more elements that come into play. While some customer journeys can become quite elaborate, learner journeys can be in a league of their own. In fact, it's quite a challenge to keep the map as simple and compact as possible without oversimplifying the learning experience.

An experience map is basically used to analyze the current customer experience so you can figure out what can be done better. This also works for existing learning experiences. But what if you want to design a completely new learning experience? Then it becomes a design tool. It is a great way to visualize your design and anticipate things that could go wrong in real life.

When you map a learning experience, the *learner journey* becomes visible. It's obvious that mapping a customer experience and a learning experience are not identical. Still, there is a lot we can learn from experience mapping for education. If you are willing to experiment and add or alter a couple of bits and pieces, you'd be able to map out learning experiences.

How to map a learning experience

First you need to know whether the task is to analyze an existing learning experience or to design a new one. Because of the innovative nature of my work as a learning experience designer, I primarily design new experiences. While this requires a bit of a different approach than analyzing an existing situation, you can follow the next steps in both cases. When you create a new experience, however, you'll probably be going back and forth between steps 2, 3, and 4 as you iterate your design.

1. Do your research

The creation of a learner journey always starts with doing research. Especially when you analyze an existing experience, it's all about researching the people who take part in this experience for what they do, what's on their mind, and what they learn. When you design a new experience, it's just as important to get to know the people and the learner in particular.

2. Create an outline

A learner journey is structured on a horizontal axis and a vertical axis. We'll start with the horizontal axis, which represents time.

Structuring your learner journey starts with mapping the different phases that take place. This offers a rough structure for you to work with. You can add details later. Be aware that all phases need to be included, including the ones that are not specifically about learning activities. Let me give you an example.

Let's say someone is looking to take an online course. The first phase, before registration, is where the person has to make a choice. The second phase would be starting the course, which could involve things like a financial transaction, registration, and creation of a profile page. These are not deliberate learning activities, but they are vital parts of the learning experience.

That said, most phases should have a learning outcome. This describes what the learner gains from each phase and how it is relevant and meaningful to them. In each phase there will be different activities. By doing these activities the learner should be able to reach the learning objectives that are necessary to achieve the desired learning outcome. Once you can write down the different phases chronologically, you get an outline of the learner journey.

3. Pick the elements you need

Now it's time for the vertical axis. The vertical axis displays elements that play a part in the learning experience like the people who participate, the activities they do, and the location where the learning takes place.

Some basic elements of a customer journey are channels, touch points, and what your customer does, thinks, sees, and feels. I like to use elements from the LX Canvas like the learning outcome, learning objectives, people, location, resources, and activities. You're free to add any element you need to complete your map either from the LX Canvas or from the customer experience mapping.

One thing I urge you to include is the emotional state of the learner. What the learner feels is a vital part of the experience as it has a huge impact on how and what we experience.

You'll want to list the different elements you choose in a way that is logical and practical. For instance, when you have different types of people, like a student, a teacher, and an external expert participating in this experience, you want to keep them close to each other so you can easily oversee their interaction. Or if you use just one location most of the time, move it to the bottom as it doesn't add much information to the journey.

4. Finalize your map

Once you've chosen all the elements you need and the different phases are clear, it's time to map out the complete experience. With the horizontal and vertical axis in place, you end up with a grid. Each spot in this grid tells you what happens at a specific moment in time.

As you start to fill up the grid, you'll see the experience in more detail. This is when you'll probably find out what may or may not work in this experience. Remember that all elements are interdependent. So you may find out that the location isn't ideal for a certain activity or that the emotional state of the learner requires that more time be taken to create the right circumstances to learn.

That's the key purpose of creating a learner journey: getting critical insights into the process the learner goes through and how all different elements impact this experience. And when you change one thing, other elements can also change because they are related.

You can make a learner journey as big or as complex as you want or need, as long as it serves the purpose of getting a clear overview of the actual experience as it takes place over time.

Experience map examples

The learner journey I'd like to show first is for a project that was designed for students in secondary education on the topic of informal care (**FIGURE 7.8**).

If you have a family member who needs care, it impacts your life. Being young and having to take care of your chronically ill mother, alcoholic father, or disabled brother is hard. Talking about it isn't easy, and that's why we designed this learning experience.

This project is also featured as a case study in Chapter 8, "Case studies." Right now, I want to focus on the way we mapped the experience. For more details on the project, skip ahead to the next chapter.

There are three things that are crucial in this map:

- First, it consists of unique and diverse activities like improvisational theater and playing a board game. Each activity is tailored for this experience, and everything needs to work together.

- Second, there are all kinds of emotions that come into play and mapping them out is essential. Dealing respectfully with both positive and negative emotions is necessary for students to grow.

- Third, timing is key as students need time to process everything and proceed when they are ready. The order and duration of activities was carefully thought out and tested.

This experience map is relatively simple and can be made rapidly. Having it enabled us to show our client, teachers, and students what the experience would be like. This gave us valuable insights for designing the activities in detail and finalizing the design.

Let's continue with the AkzoNobel e-learning example about color theory discussed earlier. We mapped out the experience for Clarissa and Daniel (**FIGURE 7.9**). They have different experiences as Daniel is eager to get started while Clarissa is less excited.

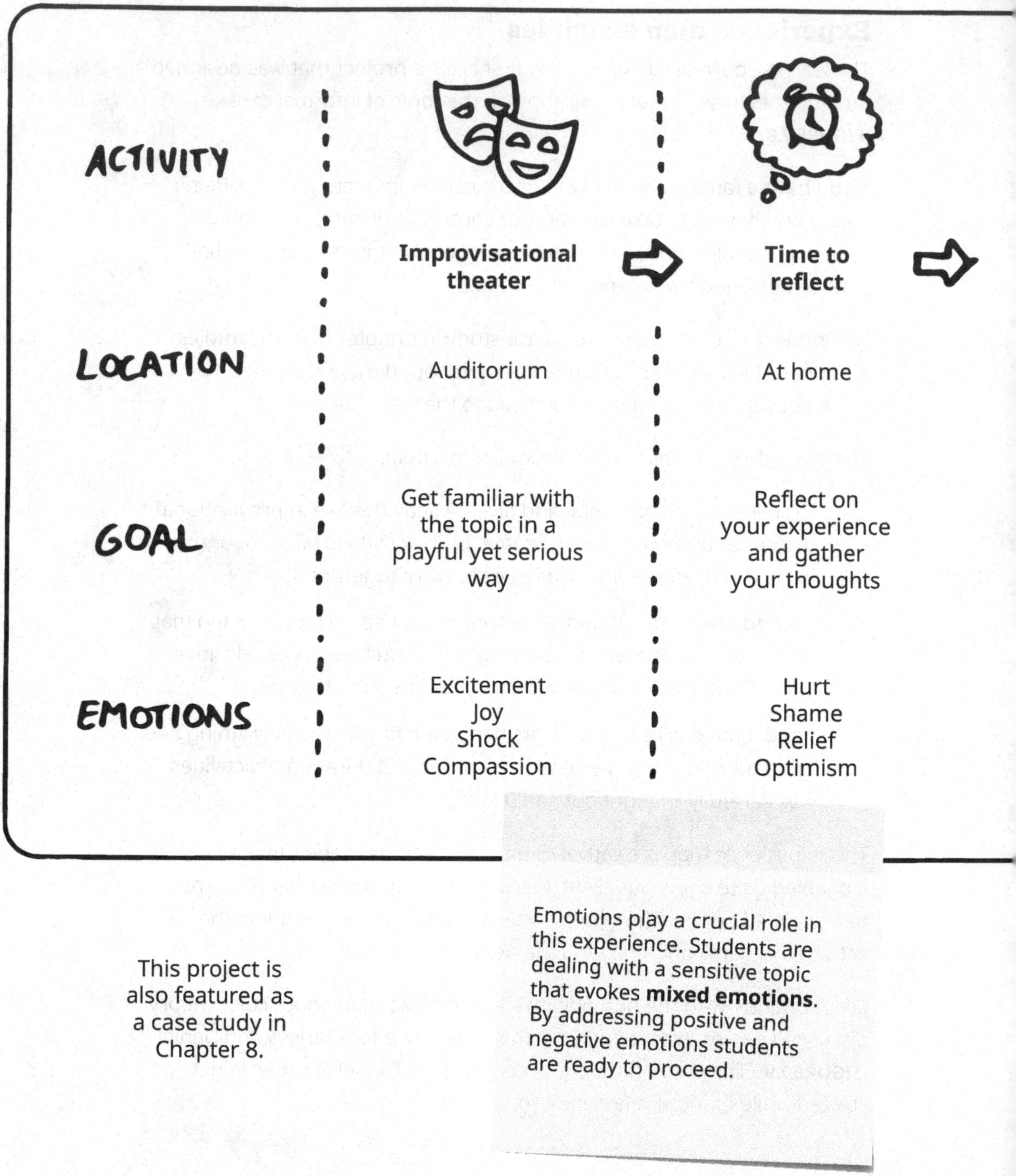

ACTIVITY	Improvisational theater	Time to reflect
LOCATION	Auditorium	At home
GOAL	Get familiar with the topic in a playful yet serious way	Reflect on your experience and gather your thoughts
EMOTIONS	Excitement Joy Shock Compassion	Hurt Shame Relief Optimism

This project is also featured as a case study in Chapter 8.

Emotions play a crucial role in this experience. Students are dealing with a sensitive topic that evokes **mixed emotions**. By addressing positive and negative emotions students are ready to proceed.

FIGURE 7.8 *Experience map for project to support young caregivers.*

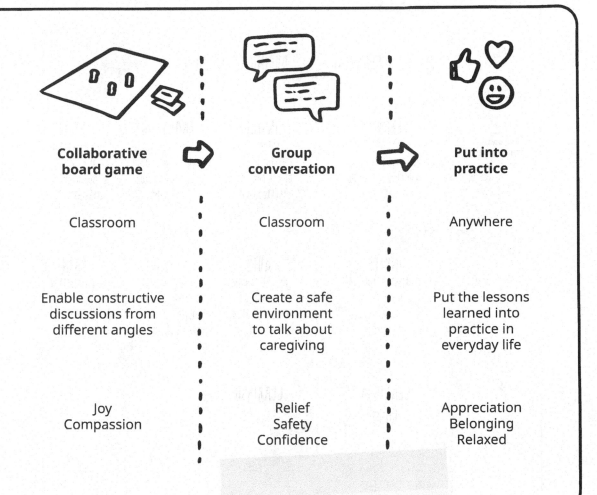

**Collaborative
board game** ➡ **Group
conversation** ➡ **Put into
practice**

Classroom   Classroom   Anywhere

Enable constructive
discussions from
different angles

Create a safe
environment
to talk about
caregiving

Put the lessons
learned into
practice in
everyday life

Joy
Compassion

Relief
Safety
Confidence

Appreciation
Belonging
Relaxed

In the second part of this
experience there is a focus on
positive emotions. For
example, students have fun
playing a board game that
they can win by working
together.

LEARNER JOURNEY

PATH	BEFORE E-LEARNING	DURING E-LEARNING		
LEARNING OBJECTIVES	**BEHAVIOR** I ONLY DO THIS BECAUSE I HAVE TO AND I'M NOT LOOKING FORWARD TO IT	**INSIGHT** COLOR IS AN ESSENTIAL PART OF OUR DAY TO DAY SURROUNDINGS	**KNOWLEDGE** I KNOW WHAT COLOR IS AND UNDERSTAND DIFFERENT COLOR SYSTEMS	**SKILL** I AM ABLE TO MIX PRIMARY, SECONDARY AND TERTIARY COLORS
ACTIVITIES	**INVITE** CLARISSA IS TOLD TO SIGN UP FOR THE E-LEARNING MODULE BY HER BOSS	**QUIZ** ANSWER FUN AND UNEXPECTED QUESTIONS ABOUT COLOR	**SCIENCE** SEE HOW LIGHT, OBSERVER AND OBJECT DETERMINE THE COLORS WE SEE	**PAINT** USE DIFFERENT PAINT CANS TO MIX SPECIFIC COLORS
PEOPLE	CLARISSA BOSS	CLARISSA		
EMOTIONS	UNEXCITED	SURPRISED	CURIOUS	
MEDIA		COMPUTER		
LOCATION	OFFICE	HOME		

FIGURE 7.9 *Experience map for an e-learning project.*

				AFTER E-LEARNING
BEHAVIOR I AM AWARE OF THE PERSONAL AND CULTURAL MEANING OF COLOR	**INSIGHT** COLOR WE SEE IS NOT STATIC BUT INFLUENCED BY MANY FACTORS	**KNOWLEDGE** I KNOW HOW WE PERCEIVE COLOR	**SKILL** I AM ABLE TO IDENTIFY WARM AND COLD COLORS	**BEHAVIOR** I AM EXCITED ABOUT COLOR AND I WANT TO SHARE THIS WITH OTHERS
PHOTO TAKE A PICTURE OF AN OBJECT WITH A COLOR YOU LOVE AND SHARE IT ON THE INTRANET	**INTERIOR** PLAY WITH THE CIRCUMSTANCES IN AN INTERIOR TO SEE HOW COLOR CHANGES	**SCIENCE** STUDY EXAMPLES OF FACTORS THAT INFLUENCE PERCEPTION OF COLOR	**SLIDER** USE A SLIDER TO SEE THE EFFECT OF WARM AND COLD COLORS	**INVITE** SPREAD THE WORD AND GET COLLEAGUES TO SIGN UP FOR THIS E-LEARNING COURSE
				CLARISSA COLLEAGUES
HAPPY				EXCITED
CAMERA INTRANET				
OUTSIDE	HOME			OFFICE

I've included Clarissa's learner journey. This is a more detailed map compared to the previous example. You can see the path, learning objectives, activities, people, emotions, media, and location.

In this case, the learning objectives are leading. The main learning objectives are included. Every learning objective can be divided up into smaller learning objectives, but that's too much detail for this map.

As you can see, there are two sequences of insight, knowledge, skill, and behavior. This is in line with the principles of experiential learning. It's not just about knowledge and skill but also about expanding their views and changing behavior. When you look at Clarissa's behavior before and after the e-learning, you can clearly see the difference.

The path provides a general structure for the learning experience. The activities enable the learner to complete the learning objectives. People are positioned between activities and emotions. This way you can see what they do and how they feel. The goal is to go from unexcited to excited in Clarissa's case. At first, she is unexcited as she is told to do the e-learning course by her boss. If we succeed, she is excited when she's done. One of our goals with this design is for learners to spread their excitement and have colleagues sign up because they are curious about this course.

The people, media, and location don't change frequently; that's why it's relatively empty. You should only add or remove things that change so you don't have to repeat the same thing every time.

When you look at this learner journey and the previous example, it's clear that there isn't one definitive form for learner journeys. Just like every experience is unique, every learner journey has its own unique form. It's up to you to find the form that works best for your design.

■ The right tool for the job

Tools are useful for any professional. Picking the right tool for the job requires experience. Using that tool effectively requires even more experience. Any of the tools that are discussed in this book take time to master.

It's easy to underestimate the versatility and depth of the LX Canvas, personas, empathy maps, and experience maps. As excited as I am about these tools, they are far less important than the person using them. A good tool in the hands of a bad designer won't make much of a difference. You get out of these tools what you put into them. Use them to apply and develop your design skills. Get creative to get the most out of them.

To design is much more than simply to assemble, to order, or even to edit: it is to add value and meaning, to illuminate, to simplify, to clarify, to modify, to dignify, to dramatize, to persuade, and perhaps even to amuse. To design is to transform prose into poetry.

—PAUL RAND, DESIGNER

Chapter 8

Case studies

WHERE IT ALL COMES TOGETHER

A great way to learn about learning experience design (LXD) is to see how it's applied. That's why I've included three case studies that illustrate the application of LXD.

The case studies in this chapter show how the design process takes place and how the Learning Experience Canvas (LX Canvas) is used. Although I covered them in separate chapters, you will see how the LX Canvas and design process are in fact inseparable.

Each case study follows the steps in Chapter 5, "How to design a learning experience:"

- Question
- Research
- Design
- Develop
- Test
- Launch

As we go through the design process, different elements of the LX Canvas will be addressed. Not all elements are mentioned in each case. I want to highlight the most significant ones to explain the key moments and decisions in the design process.

These case studies are about three totally different kinds of learning experiences. This displays the diversity of LXD and the versatility of the LX Canvas. All cases are designed by myself and my team at Shapers.

Case 1: E-learning

How do you transform traditional e-learning about a dry topic into an exciting learning experience? That's what this first case is about.

What are the consequences when a bank employee provides a loan to an organization that launders money? Or to an organization that appears to be financing terrorism? This causes serious damage to the bank and society.

To prevent this, we were asked to redesign an e-learning module on the topic of anti-money laundering and combating the financing of terrorism (AML-CFT) for an investment bank. Their employees need to know exactly what to look out for and what to do if they suspect risks.

For this topic, up-to-date knowledge is essential but not enough. We wanted to focus on the *behavior* and *actions* that can keep this bank and their clients safe.

As an international financial institution, the bank is continuously engaged in the professional development of its employees. E-learning plays an important role in this. Of course, we are not an e-learning agency but rather learning experience designers. We decided to push the boundaries of e-learning in order to deliver a memorable learning experience.

Our approach turned out to be fundamentally different from what they expected. In addition to meeting the identified challenges, this approach also produced noteworthy results. Close collaboration and good guidance during the creative process were proven to be indispensable.

Question

Can you redesign our e-learning module about anti-money laundering and combating the financing of terrorism (AML-CFT) to make it more engaging, appealing, and effective?

What the client needs

We need our 3,000 employees to act decisively when they suspect possible money laundering or financing of terrorism.

Learning outcome

In the learning outcome we formulated how the learner would think, feel, and act after completing the e-learning course.

I feel confident about my ability to contribute to the fight against money laundering and the financing of terrorism. In this fight the consequences of making the wrong choices or not taking action can be immense. That's why it feels good to know that colleagues and I are alert, ready, and able to take action when needed.

Research

AML-CFT is a challenging and important topic. The previous module was content heavy and quite theoretical. That's why we researched situations bank employees encounter, to figure out what they need to learn in order to identify threats and prevent money laundering and the financing of terrorism.

 Learning objectives

Behavior
I am alert and pro-active at all times because we, as employees, are the first line of defense for AML-CFT.

Insight
I see the threat of money laundering and financing of terrorism is real. It can harm me, my organization, and the world around us.

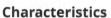

Skill
I will raise a red flag when I suspect there is a threat. If my suspicions are correct, I can act straightaway.

Knowledge
I understand the process of money laundering and know how it is used to finance criminal activities and terrorism.

Characteristics
In a financial institution with more than 3,000 employees you will find different kinds of people. At the same time, there is overlap when it comes to the level of education and the industry they work in. We decided to focus primarily on newcomers who aren't familiar with the subject while keeping it fresh for more experienced employees.

Design

E-learning can be boring, we know! That's why this design is different. We came up with an interactive story that unfolds with each step you take and each choice you make. This highly interactive approach makes everything more realistic and actionable. It also enabled us to take the infamous Next button out of most of the e-learning module.

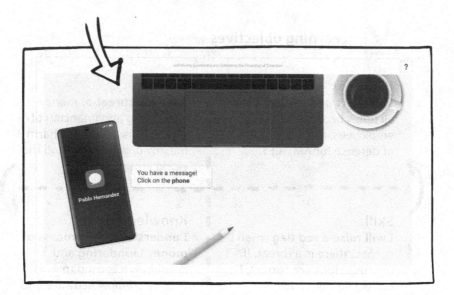

You have a message!
Click on the **phone**

Pablo Hernandez

Develop

We created a prototype in two steps. First, we created a storyboard using Adobe XD and Adobe Illustrator to create a clearer picture of what the e-learning module would look like.

Second, we made an interactive prototype using Articulate Storyline 360. In this case, Articulate Storyline was required by the client, making it both a **resource** and a **constraint**.

Test

While we couldn't travel to the client at the time, we did have access to learners for our user tests. We used virtual contextual observation as the learners interacted with the prototype.

The test results were clear: they enjoyed the novel design and hands-on approach, but they could use a bit more support to get started. Not having a Next button took some getting used to.

Due to the unconventional nature of the design, we developed several prototypes and conducted a second round of testing after we had incorporated some improvements.

Launch

After multiple iterations, meetings with the client, and two user tests, we were ready to launch. Of course, we had to provide a SCORM file for the module to be added to their learning management system. This needs to be done and checked carefully to ensure everything works perfectly.

Results

We were eager to know what the learners thought of our design. Their feedback was overwhelmingly positive:

> "The course was very interactive and stimulating. I actually had fun doing it, which I did not expect."

> "I've done dozens of these topical online courses in my life, and this one was truly the best I've ever seen. The concept is amazing, and the delivery is top notch!"

> "Congratulations because it is not easy to create an entertaining course about such a matter. I had fun."

Learners enjoyed completing the e-learning module and appreciated the way the subject came to life. Those who had done the previous, more traditional module were pleasantly surprised and clearly preferred this design over the old one.

Lessons learned

This was the first project for a new client. Our decision to create a rather unconventional design was met with some resistance. We transformed their resistance into enthusiasm by choosing to:

- Involve the client in the design process.
- Share user test results with the client.
- Deliver a tested learning experience that was highly valued and enjoyed by the learner.

Turning a content-heavy e-learning module into something special is hard. It requires a lot of time and effort from both the subject matter experts and the design team. There is a big difference between putting content on a slide and turning content into an interactive story where the choices you make impact the outcome. This was a fun challenge though and the engagement of the client and the learners made all the difference.

Case 2: Casual game

Dutch people, like me, love to cycle just as much as we love using our phones. Combining these two is a bad idea, but it happens a lot. Time to change that!

It's not hard to imagine how using your phone while cycling is a bad idea. Being distracted increases the chances of an accident significantly. In that regard, teens are a vulnerable group as they ride their bikes daily but generally underestimate danger.

That's why the Dutch traffic safety organization decided to do something about it. They invited us to come up with a playful learning experience that aimed to change this behavior. Our design is part of a lesson package they are already offering to schools.

It may sound contradictory, but we found the solution in the source of the problem: their phones. If teens are glued to their screens, that's where we can best reach them. And if they prefer to do something they love, like playing a game, we can use that to our advantage.

That's why we came up with Wheelie Pop. It is a casual game that is a fun solution to a serious problem.

Question

How can we prevent teens from using their phones while cycling?

Learning outcome

I know it's a bad idea to use my phone while cycling. I'll try to keep my phone in my pocket and ignore alerts for messages. It's not easy, but I'm determined to spend less time using my phone on my bike.

The science of impulse control

How do you train impulse control? That's what a group of Dutch scientists from Radboud University wanted to research. The answer: stop signal treatment (SST).

The concept of SST is to train reacting to the right, and ignoring the wrong impulses. This is trained by rapidly showing images where you have to choose quickly if you are going to react or not. By repeating this process, you become better at ignoring wrong impulses while acting on right impulses. That's perfect for achieving our learning outcome!

Research

The two primary things we researched were the learning objectives needed to reach the learning outcome and the characteristics of the learner. We had research on how to train impulse control. Let's look at the learner and figure out who they are, what they need, and what they would prefer.

Characteristics

"I know it's dangerous to use my phone on my bike, and others get into accidents, but that won't happen to me." This summarizes the challenge we face. A teen brain is able to identify a risk. Teens generally underestimate risks and overestimate their own abilities. They can try stupid things because they feel invincible. Their desire to have fun, and their risky behavior are two key characteristics for these learners.

Strategy

If they want to have fun and take risks, we could make a challenging game with a sense of humor.

Learning objectives

Looking at the characteristics of our learner, they understand there is risk in their current **behavior**; they just don't act to reduce it. It's also clear that lecturing them by offering more **knowledge** is not going to change much. They're not impressed if you tell them the chance of getting hurt is 40% higher when you use a phone. Those are just numbers.

That's why we focus on strengthening the **skill** of impulse control. At the same time, we want them to be aware (**insight**) that it is simply hard to do several things at the same time.

Design

Game design consists of various elements like characters, levels, rules, storytelling, game mechanics, and a user interface. Every part needs to be well executed, and everything needs to work together. We wrote a funny plot about an evil CEO of a phone company who hypnotizes teens to get them addicted to their phones. You have to resist using your phone, catch the CEO, and save your friends. SST was used as the primary game mechanic. By adding the right look and feel, we created the fun mobile game Wheelie Pop.

Develop

For the development of the game we used Unity for iOS and Android. Unity enabled us to create prototypes relatively quickly, which is vital because game development requires a lot of testing. All visual elements were created using Adobe software.

Test

As mentioned, game design involves frequent testing. From early prototypes to the final design, you need confirmation of the many design choices you make. We went to schools to test with students and used contextual observation. Seeing them play the game and capturing their honest reaction and emotional response produced significant insights.

One thing we learned is that for some students the game was too challenging while others had no problems reaching new levels. Unfortunately, we didn't have te time or money to improve that before the launch which is a **constraint**.

Launch

The launch of this project took place at a school where a Dutch YouTube star challenged a group of students for the high score. Having such a lively event and social media coverage was essential to get teens playing. Creating awareness is an important first step if you want to reach students around the country.

Results

There are various ways to determine whether this project was successful. The most important question is whether teens who played this game changed their behavior. The answer is yes, kind of. The effectiveness of the game was assessed by a research agency. They found out that of all the players they tracked, 23% used their phone less. That number is higher for players who spend more time playing Wheelie Pop.

Knowing that you are training a skill as you play, it makes sense that it takes time and effort to see improvement. They also saw an increased awareness of the risk of getting into an accident. That's good news.

Another measure of success is how many people play and enjoy the game. Since its release, Wheelie Pop has been downloaded more than 50,000 times and gets 3.5 out of 5 stars. Overall, a success!

Lessons learned

All the way at the end of designing a learning experience, you launch your design. Often, launching your design is an afterthought. This launch was vital to the success of the project.

After the launch we added features to the game to make it easier for players who struggled, without taking away the challenge for more experienced players. We also created more levels as we know that playing longer results in better impulse control. We wanted to attract more players and to keep them playing and training.

Working with scientists has been of incredible value for this project, both for the design of this game and to measure the results. We were able to use our design skills more effectively thanks to their work.

Case 3: Serious play

One in four children grow up in a family where someone needs care. Being young and taking care of a family member is common but rarely talked about.

Being a caregiver has a big impact on people's lives. Especially when you are a child, it can be tough. If you have to take care of your chronically ill mother, alcoholic father, or physically impaired sister, you are going to miss out on a lot of things. As a result, these children often feel misunderstood or lonely.

On November 10 in the Netherlands there is a national day for informal care ("Dag van de mantelzorg"). It spotlights people who voluntarily take care of someone close to them. In honor of this day, we were asked to design a learning experience specifically for young caregivers.

Our goal is to bring awareness to the topic and find ways to deal with the challenges for the caregivers, their friends, and the ones receiving care. Together with event designer Hanneke van den Broek we came up with a couple of unique activities that take place primarily in school.

This project is also featured as an experience map in Chapter 7, "Design tools." You might want to flip back to that part to see the experience map.

Question

How can we bring the sensitive topic of young caregivers out in the open at school in a **thoughtful** and **meaningful** way?

Learning outcome

Caring for a family member as a student is challenging, and not being able to talk about it is hard. Opening up about such a sensitive topic requires a supportive and safe environment.

Talking about a topic is not enough; you want this learning experience to help tackle the challenges faced by young caregivers, the ones receiving care, and their classmates.

Research

We were shocked to hear that one in four teens is a caregiver. The fact that this topic is rarely talked about, even though it is so common, is baffling. Our client was able to provide us with valuable input for the design process. Having designed several other learning experiences for Dutch students in secondary education made it easier to empathize.

Young caregivers generally miss out on things because of their situation at home. Feeling regret, shame, loneliness, sadness, and frustration is a common **characteristic**.

Learning objectives ·····

Behavior
When a classmate is a young caregiver or receives care, **I am sensitive** to their needs and **willing to help**.

Insight
I am aware of the fact that many students take care of family members. Some of my classmates probably do.

Skill
I am able to openly and respectfully talk about this topic and help tackle real-world challenges.

Knowledge
I know about the different situations young caregivers are in and the challenges they face.

Strategy
If this is a common situation, we need to assume there are young caregivers or students receiving care in each classroom. That's why we need to give them time to decide if and when they want to open up about their situation.

Design

We knew we had to do something special for this project. The topic is sensitive and young caregivers are in a vulnerable position. We are dealing with a range of emotions, unawareness, and misconceptions. We mapped out a learner journey with that in mind. You can find that learner journey in Chapter 7.

Activities

We designed three activities: Improvisational theater, a board game, and a group discusssion. The **location** for the theater was the school's auditorium. We used a classroom for the board game and discussion. These provided suitable **environments**.

Photo courtesy of Pjotr Wiese.

Process

Making these activities work well together requires the right timing. We designed the process in a way that allowed students to take it step by step and participate on their own terms. They have time to reflect and process their experience before moving to the next activity. This is essential for gradually moving towards the learning outcome.

Develop

Prototyping this experience is complicated. Each activity needs to be developed separately, yet everything has to work well together. Actors need to be briefed, the board game needs to be created, and the teachers need instruction and tools for the classroom discussion.

Test

We were not able to test the complete experience before launching it as a pilot. In a way, the pilot is the ultimate test. We did test the board game multiple times during development. Even a quick test with colleagues can be very insightful.

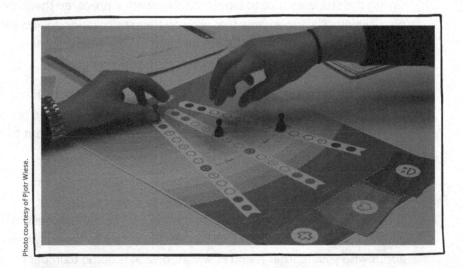

Photo courtesy of Pjotr Wiese.

Launch

Launching a pilot is always exciting and a bit scary. You have to trust your design skills, come well prepared and see if things turn out the way you intended them. Also, you need all parties to be on board and ready to make the experience a success. I've learned that if you put in the work and design with empathy and care, things almost always work out.

Results

This pilot launched at a couple of schools. The goal of openly and respectfully discussing the topic of caregiving was achieved. In that regard, both we and the students succeeded.

The introduction of the topic through theater broke the ice and sparked curiosity. It was a bit uneasy at first for most students, but that changed quickly. We are aware that this activity is quite unexpected, and there can be initial hesitation or a bit of fear to overcome.

Giving the students time to digest this experience prepared them for the next activity. Playing a game that allowed them to collaborate and see things from different perspectives enriched the learning experience. The game worked well, but there was room for improvement.

By the time the teacher opened a discussion in the classroom, most of the students were ready for it. They were able to take what they had learned and put it into practice. Overall, we accomplished what we set out to do.

Lessons learned

Trying new things pays off if your intentions are clear and honest. When you do something out of the ordinary, it's important to carefully think about who your learner is and how your design is going to impact them.

Although this project was successful, it wasn't adopted on a larger scale. There are several possible reasons for that. First, this topic isn't a priority for many people or schools. Second, we are asking quite a lot from the schools and the students. Our approach is not a simple solution that is quickly implemented. Instead, it is a unique design that takes time and effort to launch effectively. Third, the scalability is limited. You need qualified actors who are prepared specifically for this project. In addition, producing board games is quite expensive unless you are working on a really large scale.

The solution could be a redesign that is easier, quicker, and cheaper to implement. The biggest challenge is not to lose the strength and unique character of this design when creating a redesigned experience.

Finally, this project was done with a small budget and in limited time. The reason I want to point this out is because of common misconceptions surrounding learning experience design. You might think that designing a unique experience is going to be costly. It clearly doesn't have to be. Being resourceful goes a long way. Also, it is often assumed that it takes too much time to do something out of the ordinary. You might settle for a standard solution with an average experience to save time. This project shows that you can do a lot in little time. I believe limitations can boost creativity and lead to amazing results.

*Sometimes it's the journey
that teaches you a lot
about your destination.*

— DRAKE, MUSICIAN

Chapter 9

What's next?

ON YOUR LEARNING JOURNEY

You made it to the final chapter. We've covered
a lot of ground on what LXD is, how it works,
and why it matters. Now it's time to think about
what's next for you!

Any experience will change you, often in a very small way and sometimes
in a big way. I truly hope reading this book has brought about a meaningful and lasting change. How you've read this book and what you've
learned from it will be different from the next person. That's why it's good
to take a couple of minutes to think about what you've learned and how
this has changed you.

Take a sheet of paper and list your main takeaways from the book. Maybe
your perception of LXD has changed drastically. Or perhaps you've discovered new tools that enable you to work differently. Write down what
comes to mind and don't overthink it. Try to approach it as a brainstorming session to get the most out of it.

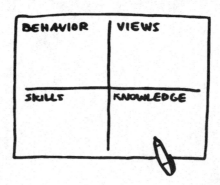

When you're finished, it's time to take a closer look. You can use another sheet of paper that you divide into four equal parts. Use these parts to analyze what has changed in your views, knowledge, skillset, and behavior.

By categorizing what you've learned, you create an insightful overview. Maybe you've acquired new knowledge, but your behavior hasn't changed. Or perhaps you've expanded your skillset without changing your views. Ideally, you want to see change in all four aspects.

Ask yourself:

- Did you gain new insights that have changed your views?

- Has the knowledge you acquired changed the way you think?

- Do your new skills support a new way of working?

- Has your behavior changed in a way that enables you to do things differently?

This exercise is about being aware of what you've learned and how you've changed. If you feel that one or more areas are lacking, you can easily see what to work on.

Your lessons can be inspirational for others. Please share what you've learned on social media using the hashtag **#lxdbook** in your post. Look for what others have posted as well to learn from each other.

Tough questions

As you continue your journey in LXD you are likely to get some tough questions from clients, colleagues, bosses, and others. Many of you have reached out to me with questions you struggle to answer.

In this section I answer several common questions about LXD in the hope it might be helpful to you when you are faced with similar questions.

Just as LXD has evolved, so have I. If you had asked me these questions ten years ago, I would have had a harder time answering them. Back then few had heard about LXD, and if they did, they just wanted to know what it was. As more people discovered it, different questions arose.

The fact that so many people are talking about LXD is a good thing. At the same time, it can add to the confusion, as perspectives and opinions may differ. LXD attracts all kinds of people, each with their own background, profession, and personal story. The questions of a primary-schoolteacher in Madrid are different from an interaction designer in Singapore.

I may not know your story, but I hope this book and these questions will help you in finding answers and sharing your passion for designing learning experiences.

I always hire instructional designers because they work quickly and effectively. Why would I hire a learning experience designer like you?

Your answer could be: I offer a different approach, and depending on your needs, it could be a better fit. My strength is to create learning experiences that haven't been done before. If you have a challenge that requires more than a standard solution, hire me.

The company I work with specializes in e-learning. I assume they are better at developing e-learning than you are.

Your answer could be: That's possible, but their strength can also be their weakness. I design all kinds of learning experiences including e-learning. I've learned that e-learning isn't always the best solution. If you work with me, I will advise you on what kind of learning experience would be best for you and your learners. If e-learning is the best fit, I'll create something that is going to surprise you and your learners. If a different type of learning experience is a better choice, I'll be able to create that for your learners.

***What is the difference between LXD and other learning disciplines
anyway? I hear it's all the same!***

Your answer could be: On the surface there are similarities, but when
you dig deeper, LXD is fundamentally different. It might surprise you,
but LXD is not a learning discipline. In fact, it is a creative design
discipline applied to the field of learning. It uses the perspective,
methods, skills, and tools of a designer to create unique learning
experiences. LXD offers a different approach to solve similar problems
in a different way.

***I'm confused! When I look at job postings for
LXD, they are almost identical to job postings for
instructional designers.***

Your answer could be: That's true. Unfortunately,
there are lots of misconceptions about LXD, and
these job postings aren't helping. It's still new to
many, and generally people relate LXD to what
they already know, which in the United States is
instructional design.

> ## Job posting
>
> Ins~~truction~~al designer
> LEARNING
> EXPERIENCE

It's interesting that in the Netherlands, where I live, it's frequently related
to *onderwijskunde*, which is best translated as educational expertise. As a
result, you see job postings that use the term *learning experience designer*
while asking for something else. If you want to work in LXD, scrutinize
what is being offered and asked for.

***You are the only person in our learning and development team who's
into LXD, and I don't get it. Why change the way we work?***

Your answer could be: I'm really excited about LXD because it combines
my creative talents with my love for learning. I believe our organization
can benefit from it — not because it is better but because it's different.
If you are able to choose from different approaches, you increase the
chances of finding the best solutions.

I've been in learning and development for years, and I recently did a design thinking course. That's the same as LXD, right?

Your answer could be: I like the fact that you are excited about a design approach to learning. There is a big difference, though, between design thinking and being a designer. It sounds like you are serious about LXD, and if you dig a bit deeper and keep developing your design skills, you will be on the right track!

LXD is just a buzzword for something we've been doing for a long time. It's nothing new!

Your answer could be: Obviously, I disagree, but let's not get into an argument. Instead, let me show you some of the work I created, and I'd love to tell you more about the design process and share some of the lessons learned.

What path will you take?

We've already tackled some critical questions in this chapter about how LXD relates to you. There is one final question you need to ask yourself: What path will you take?

Every learner journey is unique. You pick your destination and choose the way to get there. Are you destined to be a professional learning experience designer? Or do you choose a pragmatic approach and extend your skillset? Basically, there are two paths you can choose to take.

Take what works for you

The first path is to use this book as a source of inspiration for adding valuable expertise to your current or future job. In other words, you take the ideas from it that work for you.

I've trained many teachers and trainers who like to offer more appealing, engaging, and motivating learning experiences to their students and trainees. Sometimes incorporating just one or two LXD skills, tools, or methods is enough to make a difference for the learner. For example, by choosing a more learner-centered approach, you can shift your focus from teaching to learning. This small change can have a huge impact that can be felt and appreciated by the learner.

Or you can develop your creativity by using my tool discussed in Chapter 6, "The Learning Experience Canvas." Remember that your design doesn't have to be perfect; it just has to be better than what you've done before. Improving your learning experiences a step at a time will have a big impact in the long run.

Not everybody is destined to be a learning experience designer. If you feel like parts of LXD are relevant to you, then use that to your advantage. Don't feel pressured drastically to change the way you work if your learners, users, and/or clients are happy. We need great teachers, instructional designers, educational technologists, and user experience designers just as much as we need great learning experience designers.

Go all in

The second path is to set out and become a true learning experience designer. This means you are able to provide a professional service to a variety of clients as a learning experience designer. Of course, this requires more than reading this book.

You will need to put in hours designing different learning experiences. Each design process you go through and every design you create is different. This means you need to be a versatile and all-round learning experience designer. This book will point you in the right direction, but to get to your destination, there's still a long way to go — how long depends on your current skillset. As discussed earlier, who you are or where you come from determines your strengths and weaknesses. It tells you what you might have to learn or unlearn. Take a good look at the different qualities of learning experience designers and the scope of LXD and ask yourself what you have to change in your approach and add to your expertise.

Wherever you go

Whether you are an aspiring learning experience designer or you are looking at LXD for inspiration, I hope this book serves you well. Don't be afraid to experiment and try new things. You never know where you might end up.

■ Let's go!

Reading a book is one thing; applying what you've read is something else. Only when you put words into action will you find out what they really mean.

We just discussed your path in LXD. Not everybody wants or needs to become a professional learning experience designer. If you can use a couple of things from what you've read that will improve the experiences of your learners, that's perfectly fine. Don't change things that work for you just because I might do it differently. If you are serious about pursuing a professional career in LXD, I'm happy and excited for you.

Remember that becoming a designer, or learning a new area of design, takes time and effort. There are no shortcuts, and it isn't going to be easy. It will be fun and fulfilling, though. As you continue to improve your design skills, the quality of your work will increase. This is rewarding for you and the learner.

I'm still learning every day with each design I create. I love the fact that there is no end to what I can learn. Just like musicians are never finished mastering their instruments and creating new music, a designer can always find ways to improve and create new designs.

Keep this book nearby. It is not intended to be read once and put down. Pick it up when you need it. You will face many challenges as a learning experience designer, and this book can help you tackle them.

I've poured over 15 years of LXD experience into the creation of the book you are holding right now. I hope the lessons that I've learned benefit you and support you on the way to mastering LXD. Enjoy the journey and thank you for letting me be a small part of it.

Keep learning and take care!

Index